THE DAY THE BRONX DIED

An Applause Original
The Day the Bronx Died
By Michael Henry Brown

Library of Congress Cataloging-in-Publication Data

Brown, Michael Henrry.
The day the Bronx died / Michael Henry Brown.
p. cm,
ISBN 1-55783-229-3
1. Bronx (New York, N.Y.)--Race relations--Drama. 2. Friendship--New York (N.Y.)--Drama. I. Title.
PS3552.R6947D39 -1996
812'.54--dc20 96-2540
CIP

Applause Books
211 West 71st Street
New York, NY 10023
Phone (212) 496-7511
Fax: (212) 721-2856

A&C Black
Howard Road, Eaton Socon
Huntington, Cambs PE19 3EZ
Phone 0171-242 0946
Fax 0171-831 8478

Distributed in the U.K. and European Union by A&C Black

Printed in Canada

THE DAY THE BRONX DIED

MICHAEL HENRY BROWN

PRODUCTIONS

The Day the Bronx Died had its World Premiere in 1992 at the Long Wharf Theatre in New Haven, CT, with the following cast:

BIG MICKEY . . . . Peter Jay Fernandez
MOTHER . . . . Brenda Denmark
YOUNG MICKEY . . . . Akili Prince
ALEXANDER . . . . Luis A. Laporte, Jr.
THE PRINCE . . . . Kelly Neal
BILLY . . . . Neal Huff
DANIEL . . . . Curtis McClairin
ODD JOB . . . . Troy Winbush
OFFICER BREAM . . . . Dennis Green
MR. KORNBLUM . . . . Herbert Rubens
BUTTER . . . . Dwayne Gurley
SILK . . . . Aaron Martin

Directed by Gordon Edelstein

The Day the Bronx Died had its New York Premiere at the American Jewish Theatre, New York, NY, with the following cast:

BIG MICKEY	Leon Addison Brown
MOTHER	Brenda Denmark
YOUNG MICKEY	Akili Prince
ALEXANDER	Luis A. Laporte, Jr.
THE PRINCE	Kelly Neal
BILLY	Neal Huff
DANIEL	Ntare Mwine
ODD JOB	Jermaine Chambers
OFFICER BREAM	Joseph Edwards
MR. KORNBLUM	Herbert Rubens
BUTTER	Garland Whitt
SILK	Glenn Herman

Directed by Gordon Edelstein

The Day the Bronx Died had its London Premiere at the Tricycle Theatre in the fall of 1994.

CAST OF CHARACTERS

BIG MICKEY, black, professional, in his late thirties to early forties.

MOTHER, black hard working and domestic, forty years old.

YOUNG MICKEY, black, smart, and baseball loving. Athletic, given to introspection and thirteen years old.

ALEXANDER, black, fourteen, tough teenager with a gentle side. The Errol Flynn of the community, both in looks and rakishness.

THE PRINCE, black, street tough and fifteen. The Prince is the prototype for what was to come in the 1980s and '90s.

BILLY KORNBLUM, white, Jewish, with a quick wit and thinks he knows everything. Thirteen years old.

DANIEL, black, a gifted teenage musician, and Young Mickey's friend and piano teacher.

ODD JOB, black, fifteen, a bully, and physically imposing. Like most bullies, Odd Job, when not with the crowd is quite the coward.

OFFICER BREAM, black, late thirties.

MR. KORNBLUM, white, Billy's father, and coach of the little league team.

BUTTER, black, teenager, basketball player from Brooklyn.

SILK, black, teenager, basketball player from Brooklyn.

DOCTOR, black, mid thirties.

ACT I

SCENE 1

In the dark, the sounds of a respirator and hospital intercom. Lights up on BIG MICKEY, *a black man in his late thirties. He walks onstage as if he's just been told he can follow the patient being wheeled into the emergency operating room, not further. He is trying to make sense of the unbelievable . . .*

BIG MICKEY: He's only thirteen years old . . . he never did anything vicious to anybody. They didn't even rob him . . . they just beat him for the joy of it . . . thirteen years old. And I don't know if my son will see fourteen. [*Pause.*]

It came out of nowhere. I was working in my office in our apartment when the phone rang. We live in one of those exclusive, doorman buildings in Manhattan. It's the kind of place my Mother toiled in as a domestic . . . a cook. She would find it most gratifying that my wife and I live comfortably in a building where not too long ago we would've only been able to enter through the "servants' entrance" . . . We have someone to clean . . . a nanny for our baby. I thought I was doing so well for a boy from the Bronx. Now . . . my life, or more accurately, my son's life, is spread across the tabloids and six o'clock news. [*Pause.*] He was attacked on the subway. [*Pause.*] The motive of the gang was unknown.

And I stand here waiting to hear the outcome of his operation. Waiting for him to tell me and the police who did this to him . . . if he's able. Now, as I wonder what we could have done to have prevented this from happening... my mind flashes back to the time when I was thirteen... My parents had bought a nice house in a working middle-class section of the Bronx. They thought they were protecting me from the things that were deteriorating in other parts of the city. [*Pause.*]

My father had just died. I had really admired him and I did not handle his death well at all. I thought I was handling it like a man.

MOTHER: You didn't even cry. How could you not cry? Ain't nobody studyin' you... How can you learn to be a man when you don't mourn your own father?

BIG MICKEY: My mother was the cook for the Rubenstein family. The Rubensteins of Sutton Place, that is.

[YOUNG MICKEY *sees the gift is a book. He frowns.*]

MOTHER: You like the gift Mrs. Rubenstein bought you, Mickey?

YOUNG MICKEY: It's uhh... uhh...

MOTHER: Signed by James Baldwin. Mrs. Rubinstein is good friends with him. Ain't that somethin?

YOUNG MICKEY: Yeah, somethin'...

MOTHER: Somethin' wrong?

YOUNG MICKEY: I thought maybe it would be the latest James Bond book...

MOTHER: James Bond! Boy, that's James Baldwin. That's literature. You mean to tell me you prefer some makebelieve Superman?

YOUNG MICKEY: Secret Agent...

MOTHER: Boy, you better read the message Jimmy Baldwin got for all the people. I'll put it on your desk.

BIG MICKEY: Because I straddled two worlds, I had two best friends.

ALEXANDER: C'mon, Mickey!

[ALEXANDER *runs on and joins* YOUNG MICKEY. *They dance.*]

BIG MICKEY: [*With record.*] I know you wanna leave me...

ALEXANDER AND YOUNG MICKEY: ... but I refuse to let you go...

[BIG MICKEY *stops singing. He watches the two youngsters pretend they are the Temptations. He enjoys the music, and the memory before him. As the music plays,* MICKEY'S MOTHER *comes in as they dance and starts rooting them on. The boys turn and see her.*]

MOTHER: How you doin', Alexander?

ALEXANDER: Hi, Ma'am.

MOTHER: You stayin' out of trouble?

ALEXANDER: Uh huh.

MOTHER: Are you?

ALEXANDER: Yeah.

[MOTHER *watches the boys dance as another Temptations' song comes on.*]

MOTHER: I'm off to work. The Rubinstein's are having Leonard Bernstein for dinner. [MOTHER *exits.*]

ALEXANDER: Who's that?

YOUNG MICKEY: He's that guy on the young people's concerts on TV.

ALEXANDER: Well, I didn't know.

YOUNG MICKEY: Well, now you know.

ALEXANDER: Come on, let's do another one. [ALEXANDER *begins to prepare to sing leads.*]

YOUNG MICKEY: You said it was my turn to sing leads.

ALEXANDER: I sing the David Ruffin leads . . . you've got the high voice like Eddie Kendricks . . . Now with this next record you be Eddie.

[*The Temptations "The Way You Do The Things You Do" now begins to play.* YOUNG MICKEY *pretends he is singing into a microphone.* ALEXANDER *sings the background. They dance in a synchronized manner. They are having a ball.* BIG MICKEY *is smiling, having a good time with this memory. The song finally fades.*]

YOUNG MICKEY: I'm gonna write my own songs one day.

ALEXANDER: You still writin' those lyrics? . . .

YOUNG MICKEY: Yeah, and when Daniel teaches me how to write music . . .

ALEXANDER: Man, we can get some other guys . . .

YOUNG MICKEY: Have a singing group . . .

ALEXANDER: That'll be boss . . .

[*Music fades. Lights down on the boys. They exit.*]

BIG MICKEY: The one with the bandanna wrapped around his head is Alexander . . . Alexander the Great to be exact. He was the toughest kid in the neighborhood. If you were a private house kid, and you ventured toward guys from the projects, there were only three words that could stop you from being stomped, stripped of your clothes, and forced to walk home naked . . .

[*Lights up on* YOUNG MICKEY *and* THE PRINCE. YOUNG MICKEY *is holding a baseball glove and is wearing a Pittsburgh Pirate cap.*]

THE PRINCE: Who do you know?

BIG MICKEY: And, those words were . . .

YOUNG MICKEY: Alexander the Great!

THE PRINCE: That sucker who swings through trees? You jivin' me?

YOUNG MICKEY: I'm not jivin' . . . I live around the corner from him.

THE PRINCE: Yeah, all right. You cool . . . If I find out you lyin' . . . yo' ass is grass, and I'm a lawnmower.

[THE PRINCE *walks away.* YOUNG MICKEY *stays there.* ALEXANDER *swings in with a Tarzan yell. Pushes* YOUNG MICKEY *aside.*]

ALEXANDER: [*To* PRINCE.] You got a problem?

[THE PRINCE *exits.* ALEXANDER *follows off after a laugh with* YOUNG MICKEY.]

BIG MICKEY: When I was thirteen years old, my greatest passions were baseball, Roberto Clemente, baseball... Robert Clemente... baseball. A few years earlier I discovered Clemente on a cool spring afternoon in Shea Stadium... There was a fly ball hit deep to right... Clemente glided back and made a graceful catch... the Mets had a man on third, and it looked like an easy tag up for the score... and when Clemente caught the ball the man at third started home. From deep in right field, Roberto threw a perfect strike to home plate. It was incredible... I'd never seen anything like it, by the laws of baseball he as supposed to be safe, but Roberto's arm broke the laws of baseball... Between innings, I went to the souvenir stand and bought a Pittsburgh Pirate cap... Roberto Clemente was always there for me... And so was Billy Kornblum.

[*Fade up.* BILLY KORNBLUM, *a Jewish kid of twelve, joins* YOUNG MICKEY. *He wears a Baltimore Oriole cap.* BILLY *goes to shortstop, and* YOUNG MICKEY *goes to third base.*]

BILLY: You just gotta switch with me... you gotta let me play third...

[*They mime taking ground balls. The crack of the bat can be heard and they react. Sometimes they catch the ball, at other times they react, they watch the ball go somewhere else.*]

YOUNG MICKEY: What's in it for me?

BILLY: Why you gotta be a schmuck, Mickey?

YOUNG MICKEY: I'm a schmuck who's gonna play third base for the Bruins.

BILLY: But I've got the better arm.

YOUNG MICKEY: [*Laughs.*] You start shootin' dope or somethin? Talkin' like a dope addict . . . Man, I've got an arm like Clemente. I can throw right field to home on one bounce . . .

BILLY: That's what I mean . . . your arm is too strong for third . . . but mine is perfect for third . . .

YOUNG MICKEY: But your father's has Nolan Sokol in right . . . my next best position is third . . .

BILLY: I've got four Roberto Clemente's.

[*Pause.*]

YOUNG MICKEY: How'd you get four Roberto Clemente's? I've been buying cards for weeks and I haven't got one yet . . .

BILLY: You want 'em?

[*Suddenly,* YOUNG MICKEY *dives for a ball, gets up, and fires to first.*]

BILLY: Way to go . . . So, what ya say?

YOUNG MICKEY: What about your father?

BILLY: He said it's okay if we make the switch.

YOUNG MICKEY: I want to play rightfield like Clemente.

BILLY: We need Nolan's power, and can you imagine His Fatness playing short?

YOUNG MICKEY: Okay, okay . . .

[BILLY *goes over to third.*]

YOUNG MICKEY: [*Cont'd.*] Not so fast . . . where's the Clementes?

[BILLY *goes into his back pocket and pulls out baseball cards and hands them to* YOUNG MICKEY.]

YOUNG MICKEY: Wow, this is boss, Billy . . .

BILLY: Wait a minute . . . my uncle's in there . . . gimme . . .

YOUNG MICKEY: Take 'im. I have plenty of Brooks Robinson's . . . Anyway, he's not your uncle . . .

BILLY: Is too.

YOUNG MICKEY: He don't look Jewish . . .

BILLY: Neither does Paul Newman . . . I told you, he's my mother's brother. His real name's Robinski. But he changed his name so people would think he was a goy. My grandmother and mother disowned him . . . If being a Jew was good enough for Koufax, then it was good enough for Robinski . . . even on her death bed, my mother didn't want him at the funeral . . . so the family disowned him . . . and his Bar Mitzvah was revoked.

YOUNG MICKEY: Git outta here. How can you take back somethin' that was done when he was thirteen?

BILLY: The Rabbi say it . . . and it's done.

YOUNG MICKEY: Yeah, right.

BILLY: I'm a Jew . . . you're a Methodist . . . I think I know about Jews. Hey, you comin' to my Bar Mitzvah?

YOUNG MICKEY: I don't know . . . is your grandmother gonna be there?

BILLY: She's my grandmother . . .

YOUNG MICKEY: Every time she sees me . . . "Ovey . . . the little schwartzer oodsh kevah . . ."

BILLY: That's a lousy imitation of Yiddish . . . Anyway, she's used to you now.

YOUNG MICKEY: She thinks I'm a vampire.

BILLY: Ya comin'?

YOUNG MICKEY: Yeah, yeah, yeah . . .

BILLY: Good . . . bring a gift! [BILLY *dives for a line drive, catches it, gets up and fires to second.*] All right, that's two. It's mine.

[BILLY *exits as he catches ball.* MOTHER *enters and crosses to* YOUNG MICKEY.]

MOTHER: See, Mickey, these white people don't want to live with us . . . They too good for niggas . . . We move in, they move out. Like we poison or something. So they seek a haven in Larchmont or Pelham Manor . . . where they can get away from us . . . the racist bitches! . . . Now a Jew, he be a different kind of white animal . . . Fact, he not like white people at all. Not like them Irish potato pickers or nasty-ass Eye-talians . . . No, no, the Jew be a different breed all together . . . more . . . human . . . almost . . . colored . . . Yes, Sir, the Jew, he be alright. Like us he be a ancient people . . . A people that know the truth fo' these Europeans created a new truth . . .

[YOUNG MICKEY *leaves.*]

MOTHER: [*Cont'd.*] They like us . . . a truly mystic people that everybody else is scared shitless of.

ALEXANDER: We gonna war!

YOUNG MICKEY: With who?

ALEXANDER: If you had been at the war party, instead of with those white boys . . .

YOUNG MICKEY: We had practice.

ALEXANDER: So did we. Are you a Gladiator or what?

YOUNG MICKEY: We're getting too old for this.

ALEXANDER: War is for men.

YOUNG MICKEY: You're fourteen.

ALEXANDER: You gonna war or are you turnin' into a faggot?

YOUNG MICKEY: I ain't no faggot!

ALEXANDER: Is that it? Is that what it is? You got sugar behind your ears?

YOUNG MICKEY: I ain't no faggot.

ALEXANDER: Mickey is a sweet boy . . . Mickey is a sweet boy.

YOUNG MICKEY: I'm warning you.

ALEXANDER: You got some nuts . . . then you can warn . . . but you're a sweet boy.

YOUNG MICKEY: Alexander, shut up!

ALEXANDER: I see you going to that faggot's house . . . I see you going to Daniel's house.

OUNG MICKEY: He's teaching me piano . . .

LEXANDER: He's teachin' you how to take it up the booty.

[YOUNG MICKEY *takes a step forward.*]

LEXANDER: The li'll sissy is going to try something that even the Prince won't do . . .

OUNG MICKEY: I'm gonna kick your ass.

LEXANDER: You're gonna kiss my ass? I knew you were a faggot.

[YOUNG MICKEY *rushes* ALEXANDER. ALEXANDER *catches* YOUNG MICKEY *and gives him an expert Judo flip.* YOUNG MICKEY *gets up and goes after* ALEXANDER *again. This time* ALEXANDER *twists him around and wraps his arm around* YOUNG MICKEY*'s neck.* ALEXANDER *is laughing all through this.*]

OUNG MICKEY: I'm not gonna say uncle . . . I'm not gonna . . .

LEXANDER: Okay, okay . . . you've got nuts, Mickey.

OUNG MICKEY: [*Still struggling.*] That's right, I got big nuts.

LEXANDER: So don't waste 'em on a fellow Gladiator, save 'em for the Eagles.

[*Pause.* YOUNG MICKEY *relaxes.*]

LEXANDER: [*Cont'd.*] Hangin' with that Jew-boy hasn't turned you into a chump yet.

[ALEXANDER *lets him go.*]

OUNG MICKEY: He's a good guy.

LEXANDER: Nah, they're all the same. His old man is just like the Jew my Pops works for . . . They got all the mon you know?

YOUNG MICKEY: Who says?

ALEXANDER: My Pops. Rebekoff's filthy rich. You know wl he's rich?

YOUNG MICKEY: 'Cause he works hard?

ALEXANDER: Works hard? Are you kiddin' me? My Pops, l works hard supervisin' . . . makin' sure Rebekoff's truc are loaded. Rebekoff don't do nothin'.

YOUNG MICKEY: He had to do somethin', how else could l get rich?

ALEXANDER: Tha's what I'm tryin' to tell ya. He's rich 'cau he's cheap. They're all cheap. My Moms says they're lil squirrels . . . they store away every penny like a squirr do nuts. It's all a plot, man. That's why they don't belie in Christmas . . . so they don't have to buy presents.

YOUNG MICKEY: Get outta here.

ALEXANDER: Square bizness. My Pops says they're real slic because they own all the stores where everybody el shops for Christmas. You know . . . Abraham & Straus Klein's, Alexander's, Macy's, man, they're all Jews. Eve E.J. Korvettes . . .

YOUNG MICKEY: Korvettes ain't no Jewish name.

ALEXANDER: See, that's how slick they are. My Pops says it's code. E.J. Korvettes really stands for Eight Jewish Korea Veterans.

'OUNG MICKEY: How does your Pops know that?

LEXANDER: He works for a Jew . . . he knows . . .

'OUNG MICKEY: Yeah, well . . . all I know is Billy ain't rich . . .

LEXANDER: You don't wanna believe me? Fine. We need to talk about the Eagles.

'OUNG MICKEY: There ain't gonna be no rules with those guys. Those project guys really want to hurt us. How we gonna fight 'em?

LEXANDER: Hand to hand.

'OUNG MICKEY: Whoa!

LEXANDER: Our Karate and Judo against their boxing.

'OUNG MICKEY: But you're the only Gladiator who really knows martial arts.

LEXANDER: They don't know that.

'OUNG MICKEY: Yeah, but I'll let you in on a secret . . . don't ask me how . . . but even though they're from the projects, I think they'll figure it out. Those guys get up in the morning fighting.

LEXANDER: I've been teaching you guys, and we've got time to train.

'OUNG MICKEY: Whew! Good . . . geez, now that makes sense.

LEXANDER: We've got 'til Saturday.

[*Pause.*]

'OUNG MICKEY: Saturday . . . as in the day after tomorrow?

LEXANDER: Well, it ain't Saturday next week.

YOUNG MICKEY: Why couldn't it be Saturday next week?

ALEXANDER: Don't go getting faggoty on me again...

YOUNG MICKEY: Look, Alexander, my Mother's paying a awful lot for these piano lessons... and she wouldn't war me to go and break my fingers.

ALEXANDER: She wouldn't want me to break your napp head either.

YOUNG MICKEY: Alex...

ALEXANDER: Weez bloodbrothers since we wuz l'il guys... know we're gettin' older now... but my blood is sti your blood and your blood is still mine... These her Eagles have been snatchin' pocketbooks... You kno how I hate those project kids...

YOUNG MICKEY: I don't hate project kids... they're just lik us.

ALEXANDER: They ain't just like us... They eat welfar peanut butter which they also use for glue. If I lived i the projects, man, I don't even want to think about i And stealin' from ladies who live in private houses. The don't give a shit what color you are. This is our hono We've got to teach those bums. Your mother could b next. [*Pause.*]

So... you a Gladiator... or you gonna play Jew-ba with that Jew-boy?

YOUNG MICKEY: Billy's cool.

ALEXANDER: He ain't a Gladiator, he ain't cool. We ain prejudice, he can join if he can take the initiation.

OUNG MICKEY: Alex, it's getting late...

LEXANDER: It ain't late...

OUNG MICKEY: I got piano practice. [YOUNG MICKEY *starts to leave.*]

LEXANDER: Don't forget the Vaseline.

[ALEXANDER *laughs.* YOUNG MICKEY *gives him the finger.*]

LEXANDER: You down, huh?

[*Long pause.*]

OUNG MICKEY: You're my bloodbrother, ain't cha?

[YOUNG MICKEY *walks off.* ALEXANDER *does a "Kata" and the Lights fade slowly on him. Lights up on* MICKEY'S MOTHER.]

OTHER: Mickeeeey!!!

[*Lights up on another part of the stage on* DANIEL *playing a Mozart piece on the piano. He is sixteen. He plays with great skill and love of the music.* YOUNG MICKEY *goes to his* MOTHER.]

OTHER: Where you been, boy?...

OUNG MICKEY AND BIG MICKEY: Out.

OTHER: Rumblin' and bumblin' and swingin' the streets...

OUNG MICKEY AND BIG MICKEY: No, Ma!...

OTHER: Rumblin' and bumblin' and swingin' in the streets... ain't got no time to mourn... ain't got time to cry. No, you too busy runnin' and gunnin' and lingerin' in the streets. You are going to pull yourself together an stop running in the streets.

YOUNG MICKEY: Aw, Ma...

MOTHER: Sunday morning... after church... don't you mak any plans... 'cause we are going to the Metropolita Museum...

YOUNG MICKEY: I went there with my class last year...

MOTHER: Yeah, well, you're going with me this year. Then got tickets to see *Hello Dolly!* You need some culture.

YOUNG MICKEY: I got practice on Sunday.

MOTHER: Well, you're going to miss it. See, I ain't gonn raise no little ignorant hoodlum... There's another worl out there and I'm gonna make sure you know it.

YOUNG MICKEY: I don't wanna go. I'm not a baby. Wh should I go someplace I don't want to go? [YOUNG MICKEY *starts to leave.*]

MOTHER: Mickey, get over here! Do you think you're grow or something?

YOUNG MICKEY: Daddy didn't make me do anything I didn want to do. Even at his funeral

MOTHER: Hush! Go on, you're late for your piano lesson.

[MOTHER *walks off.* YOUNG MICKEY *goes to the piano and begins to play...*]

BIG MICKEY: I enjoyed going to Daniel's... there was solace in this music that I didn't quite understand...

[*As* YOUNG MICKEY *begins playing,* DANIEL *puts his arm around him.*]

G MICKEY: [*Cont'd.*] Daniel Van Drake was the first . . . the only genius I have ever known. His real name wasn't really Van. He adopted it from his favorite musician, Van Cliburn. Daniel was in love with Van Cliburn.

[YOUNG MICKEY *notices* DANIEL*'s hand on his shoulder. He is uncomfortable, but continues to play.*

DANIEL*'s hand moves down* YOUNG MICKEY*'s back.* YOUNG MICKEY *abruptly gets up.*]

ANIEL: What's the matter?

OUNG MICKEY: What's the matter?

[*Light pause.*]

ANIEL: Oh . . . I was just encouraging you.

OUNG MICKEY: Yeah, well . . . encourage me with a little less . . . you know . . .

ANIEL: It didn't bother you before.

UNG MICKEY: Yeah, well, it bothers me now.

ANIEL: I can't touch you?

OUNG MICKEY: You ain't a girl.

ANIEL: You touch girls!

OUNG MICKEY: Not yet . . . Never thought about it . . . but it's starting to get interesting. I feel like touching them. I mean, sex and all the stuff is confusing.

ANIEL: I don't find it confusing.

YOUNG MICKEY: Like, you know, I found baseball . . . and thought that was life. What else could a guy want? No I want to touch girls . . . Guys touchin' guys . . . that seen creepy to me.

DANIEL: I'm not creepy. I see guys touch you all the time . you don't get the creeps . . .

YOUNG MICKEY: Don't no guys touch me . . .

DANIEL: On the ass.

YOUNG MICKEY: Git outta here!

DANIEL: Every time I go to one of your baseball games ar you get a hit, or make a great play, I see your tean mates . . . they pat you on the butt. Your little Jewis friend is always doing it . . . Mickey makes a great catc Billy pats him on the butt . . . Mickey gets a hit . . . Bil pats him on the butt . . . And when you guys play footba and he's the quarterback, and you're . . .

YOUNG MICKEY: All right! Okay. Drop it.

DANIEL: But why do you let them pat your . . .

YOUNG MICKEY: It's tradition!

DANIEL: Well, it's a tradition I'm totally behind. [*Pause.*] Si okay?

YOUNG MICKEY: No hands . . .

DANIEL: No hands. Continue.

[YOUNG MICKEY *begins to play a shaky Mozart Piece.*]

DANIEL: [*Cont'd.*] I've got a competition coming.

YOUNG MICKEY: You'll win.

DANIEL: You sound so sure...

YOUNG MICKEY: You can play this weirdo stuff better than anyone I know.

[*Slight pause.*]

DANIEL: You've been getting really good at reading music... and I was thinking...

YOUNG MICKEY: Yeah?...

DANIEL: Will you be my page turner?

YOUNG MICKEY: For what?

DANIEL: Because I asked you. Maybe you'll bring me luck.

YOUNG MICKEY: I don't know. I...I... [YOUNG MICKEY *continues to play. Then he stops playing.*] Can't I play something else?

DANIEL: When you learn to play this perfectly.

YOUNG MICKEY: This is boring.

DANIEL: Well, Mickey... think of your boredom as an obstacle, which has been put in your way so that you can overcome it...

YOUNG MICKEY: I've been playing this dumb song for three weeks...

DANIEL: Perhaps if you would concentrate a little...

YOUNG MICKEY: I'd concentrate a whole lot better if it was something hip.

DANIEL: Oh, like rock 'n roll? For six months I've been trying to impart to you the beauty of playing piano... Your mother wants me to cultivate you. She knows the music can make you see the world totally different. You listen to that junk and that's what your mind becomes. But I give you Van Cliburn records and what do I hear coming from your house? The Beatles.

YOUNG MICKEY: Jimi Hendrix! I haven't played a Beatles record in months.

DANIEL: [*Throws up his hands.*] What am I going to do with you?

YOUNG MICKEY: Teach me to write songs.

DANIEL: Compose? Chile, first you've got to get the basics down. Then we can talk. Anyway, are you going to compose like Mozart? No! You're going to pollute the world with Jimi Hendrix and the Beatles...

YOUNG MICKEY: I'll be your page turner at the concert.

[*Pause.*]

DANIEL: You will?

YOUNG MICKEY: But I want you to do me a favor... Seein' as I ain't ready to write my own music...

[YOUNG MICKEY *pulls out a crumpled sheet of paper and gives it to* DANIEL. DANIEL *looks at it.*]

DANIEL: What's this supposed to be? Lyrics?

YOUNG MICKEY: Right now it's a poem...

DANIEL: Okay, it's a poem. So?

YOUNG MICKEY: Write music to it.

DANIEL: Van Cliburn would disown me . . . Mozart would roll over in his grave . . .

YOUNG MICKEY: Daniel . . . please . . .

DANIEL: Well . . . I suppose it wouldn't hurt to give it a little Rodgers and Hammerstein treatment.

YOUNG MICKEY: I was thinking more Lennon/McCartney . . . or at least Smokey Robinson.

DANIEL: I will not write trash. I mean, it's been the classics since I was five, chile. I was a genius at conception, and I am a genius now at fifteen. No niggity be bop, boop boop dee doo for me!

[*Lights down on* YOUNG MICKEY *and* DANIEL.]

SCENE 2

Lights up on BIG MICKEY.

BIG MICKEY: Saturday came . . . I did not sleep the night before in anticipation of the pain that was sure to come . . . Those project guys did not play around. While we hung out in the woods pretending to learn karate, the Eagles were learning to be full time hoods. They were ripping off people for money . . . bustin' up kids who stepped on their sneakers . . . even beating up teachers in our junior high school. The Eagles were getting a reputation.

[*Lights up on* YOUNG MICKEY *as he jumps into the air, screaming as he executes a flying kick.* ALEXANDER *enters. He watches* YOUNG MICKEY *throw a kick.*]

ALEXANDER: Get that leg up higher. Higher!

[YOUNG MICKEY *kicks again.*]

ALEXANDER: [*Cont'd.*] That's the way Kato does it on the Green Hornet. That's a number one kick.

YOUNG MICKEY: Thanks . . . where's everybody at?

ALEXANDER: Thought you didn't want to fight?

YOUNG MICKEY: I'm here, ain't I?

ALEXANDER: Thought you wuz scared.

YOUNG MICKEY: Yeah . . . I'm scared.

ALEXANDER: But youse here. Why?

YOUNG MICKEY: 'Cause we been bloodbrothers since we wuz little. 'Cause I owe ya for savin' me from guys like the Prince. You know, it's gonna be worse if we beat 'em. They gonna get us alone, man. They gonna take it out on our houses . . . come over from the projects . . . and throw rocks at our windows. But I'm here see . . . Where's the other guys? Skip, Greenie-boy, Grey-man and Pablo? [*Pause.*]

ALEXANDER: They're not comin'.

YOUNG MICKEY: Not comin'? Whatcha mean?

ALEXANDER: There ain't gonna be no fight today.

YOUNG MICKEY: When we gonna fight 'em?

ALEXANDER: We ain't never gonna fight 'em . . .

[*Pause.*]

YOUNG MICKEY: What are you talkin about?

ALEXANDER: I'm moving to the projects.

YOUNG MICKEY: [*Laughing.*] Who you tryin' to psyche on? Got to do better than that.

ALEXANDER: I ain't kiddin', man. My Pops got into it with that Jew he works for. He worked for him for ten years. He just up and fired my Pops.

YOUNG MICKEY: You don't gotta move to the projects... Your Pops just got fired, he'll find another job.

ALEXANDER: Naw, man, it ain't like that. My Pops has been outta work for months... him and my Moms just didn't tell me. They was barely payin' the mortgage when he was workin'... They shoulda told me...

YOUNG MICKEY: They didn't want to worry you.

ALEXANDER: Yeah, well, I'm worried now.

YOUNG MICKEY: You're movin' to the projects?

ALEXANDER: Square bizness. My Moms says that if things don't get better we might have to get on welfare...

YOUNG MICKEY: Dag...

ALEXANDER: Yap... Anyways, we can't fight the Eagles.

YOUNG MICKEY: Sure we can. I know you're feelin' down now... but when you're feeling better, we'll get the fellas together...

ALEXANDER: There ain't gonna be no gettin' the fellas together. There ain't gonna be no more Gladiators.

YOUNG MICKEY: Why not?

ALEXANDER: C'mon, Mickey, I'm a project kid now...

YOUNG MICKEY: I don't care if you're a project kid... you're my bloodbrother.

ALEXANDER: Listen to me. I'm making a deal with the Prince

YOUNG MICKEY: You don't gotta make no deal with the Prince. You can just square off on him and beat him.

ALEXANDER: It ain't that easy. Man, you know even if I get in a fight with him it ain't gonna be fair... One of the guys in his gang will jump in if I get the best of him They ain't gonna let him lose no fight... So don't you start believin' that. Now I'm gonna make a deal with them so that you guys will...

YOUNG MICKEY: What kinda deal you makin' with those creeps?

[ALEXANDER *sees* THE PRINCE *coming.*

THE PRINCE *enters with one of his boys,* ODD JOB. YOUNG MICKEY *breaks into a Karate stance.* ODD JOB *laughs. He makes his finger like a gun and shoots. He laughs.*]

ODD JOB: That's what I got for that Karate shit. Just wait, dufus... 'cause your shit is weak. And this here's a new click. Oh yeah...

THE PRINCE: Odd Job, step back and shut up.

ALEXANDER: Back off, Mickey.

THE PRINCE: Alexander ever tell you about the time I wuz visitin' his house, and I had to go to the bathroom... so I asked his momma how to get there... and she hand me a flashlight and a bat, and said, "that way, and good luck!"

ODD JOB: Sound... sound... He sounded you down.

ALEXANDER: The Prince ever tell you about the time I went to his house for dinner... and I asked his momma what he was eatin'... and she gimme a fork and say, "First one who fall asleep!"

THE PRINCE: [*Laughs.*] Now that's a cold sound. [*Pause.*] So... what's my War Counselor ran down to me...

ODD JOB: Yeah, yeah, Alexander the Great on his knees... Make 'im kiss your ass, Prince... make 'im kiss yo' ass.

YOUNG MICKEY: No!!!

[YOUNG MICKEY *rushes toward them, but* ALEXANDER *grabs him before he can get to the* THE PRINCE. *He wrestles* YOUNG MICKEY *to the ground.* ODD JOB *and* THE PRINCE *come over.*]

ODD JOB: Hold his li'l ass down.

ALEXANDER: What?

THE PRINCE: Nobody touches The Prince in anger.

ALEXANDER: What's the debt?

ODD JOB: Six shots in the chest. Now hold him down so I can slam him.

[*Pause.*]

ALEXANDER: I'll do it.

THE PRINCE: I thought he was your man?

ODD JOB: Whoa, whoa, I'm the executioner . . . you don't come out into the Eagles giving orders.

THE PRINCE: Okay, do it. And since he wuz your main man, and I feel merciful, make it one shot.

ODD JOB: One shot? Aw, Boss, one shot . . . you lettin' this guy come in and . . .

THE PRINCE: The sight of his blood would make me happy, and it would convince me of your loyalty.

[ALEXANDER *looks at* YOUNG MICKEY.]

THE PRINCE: Hold 'im up, Odd Job.

[ODD JOB *does.*]

THE PRINCE: Do it.

[ALEXANDER *does.* YOUNG MICKEY *crumples.* ODD JOB *lets him fall to the ground.*]

THE PRINCE: If the faggot is crying, give him another, Odd Job.

ALEXANDER: But you said . . .

THE PRINCE: Shut the fuck up.

[ODD JOB *checks* YOUNG MICKEY.]

THE PRINCE: [*Cont'd.*] Is he crying?

ODD JOB: [*Laughing.*] He ain't cryin' . . . But he sure is bleeding like his momma on her period. His eye is swellin' but he ain't cryin' . . . Want me to make him cry?

THE PRINCE: Yo' man got heart.

HE PRINCE: It's time to grow up. It's time that there's some meanin' to what we're doin'.

LEXANDER: I don't understand.

HE PRINCE: It's time we get in the shit.

[ALEXANDER, THE PRINCE, *and* ODD JOB *exit.*
Lights up on the MOTHER *and* OFFICER BREAM.]

IOTHER: It's them project kids. It ain't none of our kids. They mommas don't do nuthin' but lay up in the bed all day and make babies . . . Collecting welfare while the rest of us work our fingers to the bone. Don't give they children no discipline. It's them project kids that's ruining this neighborhood.

FFICER BREAM: You're absolutely right. And we're letting them.

IOTHER: They need to drop an atom bomb on them projects. Then build some nice private homes . . . or, even better, a nice park where everybody, black and white, can have picnics together . . . But it ain't our kids. It's them project kids I tell you.

FFICER BREAM: You're absolutely right. I wish more mothers and fathers were like you. You're raising a fine boy, can hit a ball lefthanded or right. You're doing a better job than some two-parent families.

[MOTHER *looks at* OFFICER BREAM *a beat.*]

IOTHER: I do the best I can.

FFICER BREAM: I know you work all the time with those

folks in mid-Manhattan . . . and when you're not workin you're taking care of the boy . . . I know that.

[*Thet look at each other a beat.*]

OFFICER BREAM: [*Cont'd.*] I was thinkin' . . . maybe the nex time I umpire one of Mickey's games . . . uhh . . . uhh

[*Pause.*]

MOTHER: Yes? . . .

OFFICER BREAM: Maybe next time you come to a game . . . really like Mickey. He like seafood? You like seafood?

MOTHER: Mickey loves it . . . so do I.

OFFICER BREAM: Great. Maybe . . . after the game . . . w could drive out to City Island. Whatcha think?

[YOUNG MICKEY *enters.*]

MOTHER: I . . . uhhh . . . oh, hi, Mickey.

YOUNG MICKEY: Hi, mom. Hello, Officer Bream. Hey, aren' you umping the game?

[OFFICER BREAM, *looking at his watch.*]

OFFICER BREAM: Oh, yeah, I better get down there. Mickey you better hurry up, too. Game starts in a few minutes.

YOUNG MICKEY: Bye, mom.

[*Lights up on* YOUNG MICKEY, MOTHER, *and* BILLY. YOUNG MICKEY *and* BILLY *playing baseball.*]

MOTHER: Where'd you get that black eye, boy? [*Pause.*] Who beat your ass, boy?

OUNG MICKEY: No, it was Karate practice . . .

IOTHER: Karate, my ass . . . Boy, who are you kiddin'?

OUNG MICKEY: It was an accident.

IOTHER: I told you to stay out of them streets. You play your baseball with that nice Jewish boy . . . you do your music with Daniel . . . but you stay away from them hoodlums. You stay out of trouble or I'll put you away.

OUNG MICKEY: Ma, I'm gonna be late.

IOTHER: Actin' up now that your father's dead. They could have put your eyes out.

OUNG MICKEY: No problem.

[MOTHER *leaves.* BILLY *goes to third,* YOUNG MICKEY *to short. The crack of a bat.* YOUNG MICKEY *dives for a ball as* BILLY *backs him up.* YOUNG MICKEY *gets up and throws the ball.*]

REAM'S VOICE: You're out!

[YOUNG MICKEY *wipes off his uniform pants.* BILLY *comes over and pats* YOUNG MICKEY *on the butt.* YOUNG MICKEY *leaps like he's been stung by a cattle prod.*]

OUNG MICKEY: Stop it!

ILLY: What's the matter with you?

OUNG MICKEY: Nothin' . . .

[BILLY *and* YOUNG MICKEY *trot in. They both pick up bats.* BILLY *is in the On Deck Circle swinging his bat.* YOUNG MICKEY *is kneeling behind him.*]

BREAM'S VOICE: Strike one!

BILLY: Why are you going weird on me?

YOUNG MICKEY: Nothin'...I told you. Just drop it.

BILLY: This guy got a real good fast ball.

YOUNG MICKEY: Yeah, hey, he's only no hit us for six innings It could be worse. Mercifully it ends with this inning.

BREAM'S VOICE: Strike two!

BILLY: Damn right...I'm gonna break up the no hitter...

YOUNG MICKEY: Sure...

BILLY: That's right...and you're gonna knock us both in with a homer...C'mon, I'll be Brooks. You be Clemente, and we win two to one.

BREAM'S VOICE: Strike three, you're out!

YOUNG MICKEY: Looks real promising.

BILLY: Valencia couldn't hit a fastball if you paid him.

YOUNG MICKEY: Like we can.

BILLY: Watch my dust.

[BILLY *goes off to bat.* ALEXANDER *enters.*]

ALEXANDER: Mickey...Mickey!

[YOUNG MICKEY *takes notice of him, then turns away.*]

ALEXANDER: [*Cont'd.*] Are you okay?

[YOUNG MICKEY *continues to ignore him. Pause.*]

ALEXANDER: [*Cont'd.*] How's the eye?

BREAM'S VOICE: Ball one.

YOUNG MICKEY: Way to go, Billy, take what he gives you . . .

ALEXANDER: It was the only way.

YOUNG MICKEY: Take your time, Billy baby, he's tired . . .

ALEXANDER: If I didn't do it, they'da busted you up good.

[YOUNG MICKEY *turns and looks at* ALEXANDER, *then turns back to the game.*]

BREAM'S VOICE: Ball.

YOUNG MICKEY: Two and O, baby . . . good lookin' it over . . .

ALEXANDER: We moved in today. I can't believe this . . . the projects. I haven't seen my Pops for a week. He didn't help us move. When he does come, he won't be sleepin' with my Moms . . . he sleeps on the couch . . . I hate the projects.

BREAM'S VOICE: Strike one.

ALEXANDER: But I've got some good news, man. The Prince likes you. He wants you to join the new clique . . . Sez you can't fight . . . but you got heart.

YOUNG MICKEY: [*Still faced toward the game.*] You think I wanna be a Eagle . . .

ALEXANDER: Eagles are dead . . .

YOUNG MICKEY: You got that right.

ALEXANDER: I'm tellin' ya there ain't no Eagles . . .

BREAM'S VOICE: Strike two.

ALEXANDER: We gotta new name S.P.E.C.T.R.E. . . . Like i James Bond.

[YOUNG MICKEY *gets up and goes over to* ALEXANDER.]

YOUNG MICKEY: I don't believe you. Odd Job's a punk . . and the Prince is scared of you. And now you're kissin his butt. Not me, man. I'm gonna be somebody,

ALEXANDER: Whata ya mean be somebody? You tryin' to b white or somethin?

YOUNG MICKEY: You don't get it . . . That's why we'r marchin' in the South with Dr. King. To let people kno you don't gotta be white to be somebody.

ALEXANDER: Get over it. You're watchin' too much TV. Yo gonna join Spectre or what?

[ODD JOB *enters.*]

ODD JOB: He better join Spectre.

[YOUNG MICKEY *goes back to the On Deck Circle.*]

ALEXANDER: Well, are you? . . .

ODD JOB: Bust his ass . . . Let's rearrange his dooty chord after the game.

[*The crack of the bat is heard.*]

YOUNG MICKEY: Way to go, Billy.

ODD JOB: I hate white ball . . . Whitey Ford and shit . . .

ALEXANDER: Come on, Mickey, you gonna join, right?

40%
OFF*
up to $12 on
your first order
of $15 or more

OUNG MICKEY: I thought we wuz gonna try to have a singin' group.

LEXANDER: I ain't got time for no kiddie shit.

OUNG MICKEY: Yeah, I just wanna play baseball.

LEXANDER: You wanna be a faggot like your Jew-boy friend?

DD JOB: He wants to be a motzah-ball eatin', spooka-Jew.

[YOUNG MICKEY *walks away.*]

LEXANDER: Why don't you wear a yarmulke, nigger-Jew boy?

DD JOB: Rag his ass, the chittlin' and lox eatin' motherfucker!!!

LEXANDER: You ain't my bloodbrother, Faggott!!! Little pussy . . . Li'l blackeyed-bloody-nosed pussy. Mickey is a pussy. Mickey is a pussy.

REAM'S VOICE: Hey, kid, you wanna cut it?

[ALEXANDER *gives him the "finger."*]

DD JOB: Suck my dick!!!

[OFFICER BREAM *enters. He takes off his catcher's mask. He is followed by* MR. KORNBLUM, *who is wearing the same baseball cap as* YOUNG MICKEY *and* BILLY.]

FFICER BREAM: Is there a problem here?

DD JOB: Suppose there is?

LEXANDER: Yeah, what you gonna do about it?

[ALEXANDER *and* ODD JOB *laugh.* OFFICER BREAM *laughs with them.*]

OFFICER BREAM: Take you to the forty-seventh precinct an wash your mouths out with clorox.

[ALEXANDER *backs away, but* ODD JOB *stands his ground.*]

MR. KORNBLUM: Okay, Okay, Officer Bream . . . the boys wer just foolin' around. Right, boys?

ODD JOB: Man, shut the fuck up!

[OFFICER BREAM *slaps* ODD JOB.]

ODD JOB: What ya hit me for?

[ALEXANDER *pulls* ODD JOB *away.*]

ODD JOB: [*Cont'd.*] Don't you know I could get one of thos bats and . . .

ALEXANDER: Nah, man . . . he's a pig.

ODD JOB: A fuckin' cop?

MR. KORNBLUM: You didn't have to do that, Bream.

OFFICER BREAM: It's what he understands.

MR. KORNBLUM: What do you want? They're just kids . . .

OFFICER BREAM: What? Look . . . I'm not gonna stand her while some kids disrupt the game, and are disrespectfu to adults.

MR. KORNBLUM: But you don't have to get violent.

OFFICER BREAM: With that type of kid, you have to get violent. It's their language. PLAY BALL!

[*As* OFFICER BREAM *goes back to the game*, MR. KORNBLUM *stands there bewildered.* DANIEL *enters and sees* YOUNG MICKEY *at bat.*]

ANIEL: Do it, Mickey!

[*The crack of the bat is heard.* ALEXANDER *looks. Sounds of kids, parents.*]

ANIEL: Homerun! Homerun!

[ALEXANDER *smiles.* BILLY *runs in, followed by* YOUNG MICKEY. DANIEL *is jumping up and down in excitement.*]

ANIEL: Go, Mickey!

[BILLY *attempts to pat* YOUNG MICKEY *on the butt, but* YOUNG MICKEY *avoids him.*]

ILLY: You're actin' weird today.

OUNG MICKEY: From now on, pat me on the back.

ILLY: What's the matter with you?

ANIEL: Nice hit, Mickey.

[DANIEL *pats* YOUNG MICKEY *on the butt.*]

LEXANDER AND ODD JOB: [*Imitating* DANIEL.] Nice hit, Mickey. [*They laugh.*]

ILLY: C'mon, let's go to Sal and Amel's... I'm buying the chocolate egg creams.

ANIEL: No, let me buy sodas. You're the heroes.

LEXANDER AND ODD JOB: You're the heroes!

ANIEL: So how 'bout it, guys?

BILLY: Sure.

[YOUNG MICKEY, BILLY, *and* DANIEL *start to leave.*]

ALEXANDER: Mickey . . .

[YOUNG MICKEY *keeps walking.*]

ODD JOB: Bust his ass.

ALEXANDER: Who do you think you are?

YOUNG MICKEY: You guys go ahead. I'll catch up.

[BILLY *and* DANIEL *exit.*]

ALEXANDER: What's the matter with you? [*Pause.*] You walkin' away from me? . . . You forgot I've bee whipping your ass since you could remember?

YOUNG MICKEY: So what? You're gonna bully me now? Lool I gotta go.

ALEXANDER: You think you're better than me or somethin You'd rather be with your faggot friends?

YOUNG MICKEY: You'd rather be with the Prince and thi dumbo than with me.

[ODD JOB *goes at* YOUNG MICKEY. YOUNG MICKEY *steps back in a Karate stance.* ODD JOB *stops.*]

ODD JOB: You don't know no Karate.

YOUNG MICKEY: Then you should be able to wipe up thi ballfield with me.

ODD JOB: Tha's right . . . let's bust him up, Alexander.

YOUNG MICKEY: You don't need Alexander.

LEXANDER: Nah, you don't need me.

DD JOB: He don't know no Karate.

LEXANDER: Tha's right, he only knows what I taught him.

[*Pause.*]

DD JOB: Just wait, uh huh, just wait and I'm gonna do ya. Just wait.

[ODD JOB *backs off.* YOUNG MICKEY *comes out of his Karate stance.* ODD JOB *feints like he's coming at him.* YOUNG MICKEY *swings but misses.* ODD JOB *laughs and backs away.*]

DD JOB: [*Cont'd.*] Yep, I'm gonna do ya . . . do ya . . . good, good, good.

LEXANDER: [*Laughs.*] You wuz right when you said I wuz getting too old to swing through trees . . . Spectre is no kiddy gang, it's . . .

OUNG MICKEY: I don't wanna hear about no Spectre . . .

LEXANDER: But it's . . .

OUNG MICKEY: I don't care.

LEXANDER: Fuck you, man.

[ALEXANDER *pushes* YOUNG MICKEY.]

DD JOB: Bust his ass!

LEXANDER: Git outta my face . . .

[YOUNG MICKEY *begins to walk away.*]

LEXANDER: Chump! Momma's boy!

[YOUNG MICKEY *is gone.*]

ODD JOB: Whatcha let 'im walk away for? Huh, whatcha le 'im . . .

ALEXANDER: Don't worry, he'll get his . . . he's a traitor.

SCENE 3

Lights up on BIG MICKEY.

BIG MICKEY: Josh Kornblum, Billy's father, loved kids. Loved being involved with kids. Josh was not only the coach o our baseball team, he was also the leader of our Boy Scou troop, as well as coach of a girl's softball team, and he wa also . . . well . . . I think you get the idea. Josh was a mensch

[*Lights up on* MR. KORNBLUM *and* YOUNG MICKEY.]

BIG MICKEY: [*Cont'd.*] When my father died, Josh was the only grownup who didn't treat me like a kid.

MR. KORNBLUM: I guess you're tired of everybody tellin' you they're sorry about your father

YOUNG MICKEY: Every time someone says it, it makes it worse.

MR. KORNBLUM: I know . . .

YOUNG MICKEY: And then you get the really stupid grownups . . .

MR. KORNBLUM: There's plenty of them around . . .

YOUNG MICKEY: They tell you it's all right to cry. What's the big thing about cryin', Mr. Kornblum? . . .

MR. KORNBLUM: Absolutely nothin' . . .

OUNG MICKEY: I mean, dag, it's like they think I'm a little kid or somethin'... I'm thirteen years old...

R. KORNBLUM: See, if you converted to Judaism, you'd of had a Bar Mitzvah at thirteen, and you would have been a man... and nobody would treat you like a little kid because your Dad died.

OUNG MICKEY: Gee, that's boss.

R. KORNBLUM: Yeah, it's pretty neat. On the other hand, if you should want to cry... even if you're a man... there's nothin' wrong with that...

OUNG MICKEY: I don't feel like cryin'...

R. KORNBLUM: That's been established. All I'm sayin' is... When my Doris died, Billy was just a little baby, I cried. And you know, I needed that cry... It was a good cry. I mean, it was definitely up there with the great rain storms... with Noah and the forty days forty nights bit. [*Chuckles.*] So... who are they to tell you when you should cry? It's totally up to you.

[*Lights down on* MR. KORNBLUM *and* YOUNG MICKEY.]

G MICKEY: Josh Kornblum was one of the few truly sane adults in my life. At Billy's Bar Mitzvah, he gushed all over his son. He bragged about him to everyone.

[*Lights up on* BILLY, YOUNG MICKEY, *and* MR. KORNBLUM. *They all wear yarmulkes.* YOUNG MICKEY *holds a gift in his hand.*]

R. KORNBLUM: I'm really proud of you... you know that, William?

BILLY: I know, Pop . . . you've told me that fifty times . . . eve since I got outta bed this morning.

MR. KORNBLUM: You're prone to exaggeration. I've told yo only forty-nine times. [*Chuckling.*] And why shouldn't I Face it, you're great. You're doomed to be great.

[*He grabs* BILLY *and kisses him.*]

BILLY: Aw, Pop.

MR. KORNBLUM: Get outta here with your "Aw, Pop," yo may be a man today, but you'll always be my boy. Hey, I'r gonna leave you alone, but I think it's appropriate, no that you're a man, that I give you some manly advice. An I want you should listen, too, Mickey . . . Lotta guys, the walk the streets . . . they live their lives as men, and the don't know the secret to manhood. Can there really b such a thing? And if there is, what is this secret? Lott guys . . . they think if they can squeeze a girl on the tusch . .

[*The boys giggle.* MR. KORNBLUM *looks heavenward.*]

MR. KORNBLUM: [*Cont'd.*] Sorry, Doris, but he's growin up . . .

[*Back to the boys.*] Lotta guys think if they squeeze tha girl's tusch that makes him a man. It don't make hin nothin', 'cause that's not how you treat a lady. Real mer don't do that. Lotta guys think . . . 'cause they're big anc strong, that it makes them a man if you beat up every body on the block. Don't you believe it. If you're a man and you happen to be strong, then you protect those you love. This is good. But you don't be a bully . . .

BILLY: Pop?

MR. KORNBLUM: Yeah?

BILLY: Could you like get to the secret of manhood? [BILLY *looks around as if this is a secret he doesn't want anyone else to hear.*]

MR. KORNBLUM: The secret to manhood is . . . truth.

YOUNG MICKEY: Truth?

MR. KORNBLUM: It will never fail you. Be true to yourself. Be true to what you believe in. Stand up when you know you're right. Tell the truth against injustice.

BILLY: That's all?

MR. KORNBLUM: That's all? Okay, I know it sounds simple, but to live your life with truth is not an easy thing. The older you get, the more difficult it becomes to tell the truth . . . to be true to yourself. Hey, maybe it doesn't sink in now . . . and what do I know? I'm still grappling with this myself. Take this as an observation from someone who has been a man for a while.

[*He hugs* BILLY.]

MR. KORNBLUM: [*Cont'd.*] Mazeltov.

[*He kisses* BILLY. *Then he goes to hug* YOUNG MICKEY. BILLY *wipes off the kiss.*]

MR. KORNBLUM: [*Cont'd.*] Mazeltov on your Bar Mitzvah, Billy . . . Mazeltov, Mickey. [MR. KORNBLUM *leaves.*]

BILLY: Geeesh! Sorry about that.

YOUNG MICKEY: That's aright. It was actually kinda neat. Your Dad's really cool . . .

BILLY: Yeah, well, you don't have to live with him every day.

YOUNG MICKEY: You don't know how lucky you are.

BILLY: C'mon.

YOUNG MICKEY: I used to be like you. I didn't know I had it so good.

[BILLY *hasn't really been paying attention. He's eyeing the gift that* YOUNG MICKEY *is holding.*]

BILLY: So . . . are you holdin' that for me?

YOUNG MICKEY: Oh, yeah . . .

BILLY: Then let me relieve you of your burden.

[BILLY *takes it away from* YOUNG MICKEY.]

YOUNG MICKEY: I'm really lousy at picking gifts out . . .

BILLY: I'll let you know if that's an accurate assessment in about three seconds . . . [BILLY *opens the present. It is a framed photograph of Brooks Robinson. It is autographed.* BILLY *is truly blown away by this.*]

BILLY: Wow! An autographed picture of Brooks Robinson . . .

YOUNG MICKEY: I knew you wouldn't have one.

BILLY: Because he's been thrown out of the family . . .

YOUNG MICKEY: That's right . . . and I thought, what better present than an autographed picture of your uncle . . . So I sent it to Baltimore . . . I didn't really think I'd get it back in time. Heck, I didn't even know that he'd sign it. But he did, and there it is.

BILLY: This is boss, Mickey. This is the best present I've ever got.

YOUNG MICKEY: Really?

BILLY: Nothing I ever got touches this. You're the best!

[BILLY *looks at the photo admiringly. Then he puts his arm around* YOUNG MICKEY*'s shoulder and they walk off together.*]

BIG MICKEY: Billy and I were like brothers. We were not that uncommon back then in what was the called the melting pot of the world. But as time passes, as the ugliness swells around us each day, I have to wonder if the warm moments with Billy and his father are memories I've distorted over the years. Whatever is true, what came afterward I buried deeply. Very deeply. Their names were Butter and Silk . . . that's how smooth they were on a basketball court and with the girls. They came from Brooklyn by the way of the Iron Horse. They were undefeated and suave in the Big Park tournament. Every weekend they'd come, and with skill they'd destroy any team that was in their way. It was half-time . . . Brooklyn Boyz 50, Projects 43.

[BUTTER *and* SILK *stop dribbling. They go downstage to the trophies.*]

BUTTER: Another half and these trophies belong to us.

SILK: Butter, they already do.

BUTTER: And some of these fly mommies too . . .

SILK: Brooklyn Boyz done conquered the Bronx . . . kicked Bronx ass big time.

[*They slap "fives."*]

THE PRINCE: What's that?

BUTTER: Oh, he wasn't talkin' to you, Bro' . . .

THE PRINCE: 'Scuse me? . . .

BUTTER: Bro' he was rappin' with me . . .

THE PRINCE: He said somethin' 'bout Bronx ass . . .

SILK: Wasn't 'bout you, my man . . .

THE PRINCE: Oh, it wuz about my woman . . .

SILK: Hey, hey, hey . . . we was rappin' about the game.

THE PRINCE: You're wearin' an attitude.

SILK: Naw, dude, I'm wearin' a basketball uniform.

[SILK *and* BUTTER *laugh.* THE PRINCE *smiles.* ODD JOB *and* ALEXANDER *move in closer.*]

THE PRINCE: Listen, you dufus-assed-faggot-faced-in-the-wrong-borough-jive-assed-Brooklyn Pussies.

BUTTER: Whoa . . . What's . . .

[ALEXANDER *slaps* BUTTER.]

ODD JOB: Silence when the Prince is talkin'.

THE PRINCE: Dig this, I ain't cha Bro', I ain't cha man . . . and I ain't cha dude . . . I'm the Prince.

[BUTTER *and* SILK *look around the park.*]

ALEXANDER: Your teammates have been sent home courtesy of fellow comrades in Spectre. Just count the cashmere coats. This is our park.

THE PRINCE: Who am I?

SILK AND BUTTER: The Prince.

THE PRINCE: Whoa, whoa, I don't like you . . . You look like one of them brave motherfuckers . . .

SILK: Not as brave as you and the twenty dudes surrounding this park . . .

THE PRINCE: The Prince must have his court . . . Say it.

SILK AND BUTTER: The Prince must have his court.

THE PRINCE: [*Offering his hand.*] Kiss my ring . . .

BUTTER: I ain't kissin' no dude's ring . . .

[ODD JOB *kicks* BUTTER *in the back.* BUTTER *falls to the ground.* YOUNG MICKEY, DANIEL, *and* BILLY *watch.* BIG MICKEY *turns away from the action, then sees the audience and is embarrassed. He puts his head down.*]

THE PRINCE: You right, man, you can't reach high enough to kiss my ring . . . So kiss my shoes . . . the bottoms.

[ALEXANDER *and* ODD JOB *raise their canes.*]

ALEXANDER: Get on your stomachs.

[SILK *and* BUTTER *do so.* ODD JOB *stands over them.*]

ODD JOB: Hey, Prince, they lay there so nice, 'cause Brooklyn Boyz like to take it in the hiney . . .

THE PRINCE: [*Laughing.*] Nah, man, that ain't true.

ODD JOB: Oh, yeah, they do . . .

[ODD JOB *puts his cane at* SILK*'s behind and turns the cane.*]

ODD JOB: Hiney, hiney!

[SILK *moves.* THE PRINCE *kicks him.*]

THE PRINCE: Be still.

ODD JOB: You know what they call it in the joint? Round eye. See a candy-ass Brooklyn boy . . . and then pop his round eye!

[ODD JOB *touches* BUTTER*'s behind with his cane.* BUTTER *does not move.*]

ODD JOB: He likes it.

[ALEXANDER *returns with* SILK *and* BUTTER*'s shoes and trousers.*]

ALEXANDER: Y'all dig these vines?

BUTTER: Hey . . .

[ODD JOB *hits* BUTTER *with the cane.*]

ODD JOB: Shad up.

ALEXANDER: Suede playboys . . . alligator shoes . . . Shadow-striped pants.

THE PRINCE: Y'all rich Brooklyn boys. Well, we gonna donate 'em to the church for ya boys.

[ALEXANDER *tosses the clothes off.*]

THE PRINCE: Them uniforms are smellin' up my park.

ODD JOB: Get up and take them fuckin' uniforms off. What the fuck you lookin' at?

[ALEXANDER *gestures with his cane. They strip off their uniforms.* BUTTER *and* SILK *stand there in their underwear.* THE PRINCE, ODD JOB, *and* ALEXANDER *laugh.*]

ALEXANDER: That's cold, Man. Tha's cold...

[BUTTER *and* SILK *try to cover themselves with their hands.*]

ODD JOB: Take their panties so we can see some hiney...

[BUTTER *and* SILK *cover more.*]

THE PRINCE: Out with your balls.

[*Long pause.*

Then BUTTER *lets out a gut-wrenching howl. He goes after* THE PRINCE. BUTTER *is thrown down, as is* SILK. THE PRINCE, ODD JOB, *and* ALEXANDER *circle them.* BUTTER *and* SILK *are on their knees, crouched and covering their heads with their hands. They are struck with the canes in unison. Then they are beaten in a frenzy.* DANIEL *covers his eyes.* YOUNG MICKEY *tries to pull* BILLY *out of the park but* BILLY *does not allow it. The gang stops caning* BUTTER *and* SILK. *A siren is heard and a police beacon is seen reflected on the back wall. All scatter.*]

THE PRINCE: Now ain't nobody seen nothin'...and there will be no evil upon you.

[OFFICER BREAM *enters. The gang has spread apart, and away from* BUTTER *and* SILK. OFFICER BREAM *bends down to* BUTTER *and* SILK *who are dazed.*]

OFFICER BREAM: You guys alright? You need an ambulance or anything?

SILK AND BUTTER: We're fine.

OFFICER BREAM: Can somebody tell me what happened?

ODD JOB: Looks like two sweet boys havin' a orgy.

[*Laughter.* OFFICER BREAM *goes to* ODD JOB.]

OFFICER BREAM: This your idea of comedy... Did you do this?

ODD JOB: Officer... [ODD JOB *crosses his heart.*] I just got here... Cross my heart and hope to die.

OFFICER BREAM: I'm thinking a lot of people hope you die... including your Momma.

ALEXANDER: Ooooh he sounded you down.

THE PRINCE: Oinks ain't suppose to sound on nobody...

OFFICER BREAM: What did you say?

THE PRINCE: Nuthin'.

OFFICER BREAM: Yeah, you're the Prince... [THE PRINCE *smiles.*] ... Prince of pimple-faced, pre-pimp, pre-penitentiary-punks... Don't suppose you...

THE PRINCE: Had my back turned, Officer...

OFFICER BREAM: And nobody's foot found its way up your ass?

THE PRINCE: Now, officer... I look nuthin' like you from behind.

[*Laughter all around the park.* OFFICER BREAM *goes to* ALEXANDER.]

OFFICER BREAM: What about you?

ALEXANDER: I ain't seen nuthin' . . .

OFFICER BREAM: You used to be a good kid . . .

ALEXANDER: I ain't seen nuthin' . . .

ODD JOB: Tha's right.

OFFICER BREAM: I know that . . .

ALEXANDER: How you know that?

OFFICER BREAM: 'Cause you're blind . . .

ALEXANDER: Tha's right . . . blind as a bat, Officer.

OFFICER BREAM: And ignorant enough to be proud of it.

[OFFICER BREAM *goes to* DANIEL.]

OFFICER BREAM: [*Cont'd.*] You a member of the gang?

[*There is laughter from everyone in the gang.*]

ODD JOB: Ain't no faggots in Spectre . . .

OFFICER BREAM: Just wait 'til they get a hold of your ass in lock-up. What you see, son?

[DANIEL *looks around.* THE PRINCE, ODD JOB, *and* ALEXANDER *strike their canes on the ground at the same time.*]

OFFICER BREAM: You want to tell me something?

[*Canes strike the ground again.*]

DANIEL: I . . . I . . . nothin' . . . I was just passing by . . . I didn't see a thing . . .

[OFFICER BREAM *goes over to* YOUNG MICKEY *and* BILLY.]

OFFICER BREAM: Hey, I know you guys... You guys did a great job of breaking up that no hitter...

BILLY: Gee, thanks...

YOUNG MICKEY: Thanks. Officer Bream...

OFFICER BREAM: You guys play so well together... Anyway, can you fill me in on what happened here?

BILLY: Well, Officer...

YOUNG MICKEY: We were just passing by to go to baseball practice...

OFFICER BREAM: Oh, yeah, practice today...

BILLY: Officer, those kids were...

YOUNG MICKEY: You have the time?

OFFICER BREAM: 3:30.

YOUNG MICKEY: We're gonna be late for practice, Billy.

BUTTER: No man, no...

OFFICER BREAM: God damn it, get away from him.

ODD JOB: I was just helping him out...

OFFICER BREAM: Tell me, they did it, right?

SILK: Nobody did nothing, it wasn't these guys.

[ODD JOB *goes to* BUTTER *and threatens him with cane.* OFFICER BREAM *runs to them.* YOUNG MICKEY *tries to pull* BILLY *away.* OFFICER BREAM *helps* BUTTER. BILLY *pulls away and goes back towards* OFFICER BREAM. *The canes strike the ground again.*]

YOUNG MICKEY: Billy! Billy!

BILLY: What?

YOUNG MICKEY: They'll get me, too.

BILLY: Not if they're in jail.

YOUNG MICKEY: What are you tryin' to do?

BILLY: Exercise my duty as a citizen.

YOUNG MICKEY: Exercise your what? You think this here is, Dragnet or somethin?

[THE PRINCE, ODD JOB, *and* ALEXANDER *point their canes at* BUTTER *and* SILK. OFFICER BREAM *does not see this.*]

OFFICER BREAM: Tell me, so I can lock the hoodlum sons of bitches up!

[BUTTER *and* SILK *look at the canes pointing at them.*]

OFFICER BREAM: Don't you want to lock up the guys who did that? . . .

SILK: I don't remember . . .

OFFICER BREAM: I've got a witness right over there who will back you up . . . Talk to me. [*Sees* THE PRINCE*'s cane.*] You stupid lowlife punk!

[*Slowly they put their canes down.* OFFICER BREAM *goes to* THE PRINCE. *He snatches the cane and breaks it over his thigh and throws it off. He shoves* THE PRINCE.]

OFFICER BREAM: [*Cont'd.*] Look at that, he don't even bite back.

[OFFICER BREAM *goes to* BUTTER *and* SILK. THE PRINCE *reaches into his coat.*]

OFFICER BREAM: [*Cont'd.*] Talk to me! Talk to me!

[THE PRINCE *draws his pistol.* BILLY *starts to say something, but* YOUNG MICKEY *grabs him from behind and pulls him to the ground.*]

BILLY: Officer!

[YOUNG MICKEY *pulls* BILLY *out of danger.* THE PRINCE *shoots* OFFICER BREAM *six times in the back. Everyone but* THE PRINCE, ALEXANDER, *and* ODD JOB *run off.*]

THE PRINCE: You broke my cane... My cane!... You gonna come in here, in my park... my kingdom... sell some wolf tickets? I'm 'sposed to 'low this?... I'm a man. Respect me or die. My boy's standin' here... all the fly mommies... and you gonna fuck with me?... You know why you dead? 'Cause it's like my Moms say... A Nigga cop treat his own kind worse than a white paddie cop... So, see, you supposed to be dead... 'Cause a nigga who think like a white man... he a roach, and I'm Raid, mother fucker! It bees the way sometime... When you invade another man's turf... kingdom... death comes fast, natural, like a hard on.

[ALEXANDER *runs off.*]

THE PRINCE: [*Cont'd.*] Where the fuck you going?

[ODD JOB *and* THE PRINCE *run off.* YOUNG MICKEY *and*

BILLY *run on to* YOUNG MICKEY*'s house.* ALEXANDER *runs in to join them.*]

MOTHER: I thought y'all was supposed to be at practice... What's wrong?

[*They look at her. Lights down.*

BIG MICKEY *goes over to dead* OFFICER BREAM*'s body and looks at it.* YOUNG MICKEY *rises from tableau and goes to* OFFICER BREAM*'s body.* BIG *and* YOUNG MICKEY *look at each other.*

Blackout.]

ACT II

SCENE 1

Lights up on BIG MICKEY *who has a bandage on his arm from the I.V. He rolls down his sleeve.*

BIG MICKEY: About a year ago, an old friend of mine asked me if I was interested in joining the Republican Party. [*Laughs.*]

I was appalled. I was indignant. He said to me, "Hey, Brother, you and the Mrs. are doing fabulous. Isn't it time you protect your assets and join the Grand Old Party?" And he told me, quite seriously, that by remaining a Democrat I was not looking out for the best interests of my family... and, finances. I told him that I was not going to forget who I was and where I came from. He looked me in the eye, and said, "You better remember who you've become, and where you want to be." [*Pause.*]

It actually reminds me of something my Father might say.

[*Lights up on the* MOTHER. *She has* YOUNG MICKEY, BILLY, *and* ALEXANDER *sitting in front of a television set.*]

MOTHER: Y'all weren't near that park, were you?...

YOUNG MICKEY: No, Ma...

MOTHER: You weren't near that shooting...

YOUNG MICKEY: No, Ma...

MOTHER: You ran in here looking scared of something.

YOUNG MICKEY: Scared . . . No. we were just fooling around.

MOTHER: Since y'all ain't got nuthin' to do . . .

YOUNG MICKEY: But, Ma . . . we got to get to practice . . .

MOTHER: Y'all sit and watch Dr. King. It won't take but a few minutes. You may not appreciate it now, but twenty years from now you'll understand.

[MOTHER *turns TV up and Martin Luther King begins to speak. The lights go down on the kids. She and* BIG MICKEY *look at each other. Then they leave the stage as the lights come up on the boys.* YOUNG MICKEY *gets up and turns the TV down.*]

YOUNG MICKEY: Where do you think Officer Bream is now?

BILLY: Dead.

YOUNG MICKEY: You think he's somewhere?

BILLY: Wherever he's at, he ain't here.

YOUNG MICKEY: Maybe he's happier . . . Him, my father . . .

ALEXANDER: I think they're happier . . .

BILLY: You killed the cop.

ALEXANDER: I didn't kill that cop, Jew-boy.

YOUNG MICKEY: Alex!

BILLY: That's right, I am a Jew-boy.

ALEXANDER: Motzaball-motazh-cracker-eatin' cracker.

BILLY: You want to offend me, call me a kike.

ALEXANDER: I'm gonna fly you like one.

BILLY: Killer . . .

ALEXANDER: I didn't kill anyone . . . Say it again and I'll kick your ass . . .

YOUNG MICKEY: Not in my house you won't.

ALEXANDER: What are you, Jewish now, Mickey?

YOUNG MICKEY: It's better than being the Prince's flunky.

ALEXANDER: Weez bloodbrothers. Ain't nothin' change that since six.

YOUNG MICKEY: Yeah, I took a blood oath with somebody . . . but I don't think it was you.

ALEXANDER: It was me. When I whip you 'til your dooty chords hurt you'll remember it was me . . .

YOUNG MICKEY: Alexander the Great . . . that was a name everybody around here respected . . . but that was somebody else. Private house or project . . . didn't make no difference, you still coulda been Alexander the Great . . .

BILLY: How he's only great at one thing—killin'.

ALEXANDER: You keep your mouth shut . . . this here is between brothers . . .

YOUNG MICKEY: Billy's just as much my brother as you . . .

ALEXANDER: He's a Jew.

YOUNG MICKEY: Martin Luther King says we're all brothers on this Earth.

ALEXANDER: My pops says King's one too.

YOUNG MICKEY: What?

ALEXANDER: A Jew lover.

YOUNG MICKEY: At least, I ain't no murderer.

ALEXANDER: Man, I didn't know the Prince would do something like that...

YOUNG MICKEY: You messed with those guys over a stupid basketball game...

ALEXANDER: We wuz just foolin' around... it got outta hand.

BILLY: My grandmother... she told me that's what the Nazi's said when they got caught.

ALEXANDER: Shut him up, or I'm gonna fuck him up!

YOUNG MICKEY: Why are you here?

ALEXANDER: Just like you guys... I wuz scared. I didn't know what to do.

YOUNG MICKEY: They're your gang now. You shoulda stuck with them.

ALEXANDER: Mickey... I didn't want to hurt nobody...

[*Pause.*]

BILLY: Then we gotta tell what happened.

YOUNG MICKEY: What?

BILLY: We gotta make sure this Prince guy don't get away with this.

ALEXANDER: You are a fucking Dudley-do-right-dufus. This Jew-boy is gonna get you crucified, Mickey.

BILLY: My dad'll drive us to the police...

ALEXANDER: Jewish kids s'posed to be so smart, what the hell happened to you?

BILLY: You want to be a mensch again, Alexander?

ALEXANDER: I don't speak that shit, all right? . . . I don't even speak Spanish . . .

BILLY: Come with us to the police . . .

YOUNG MICKEY: Us?

[ALEXANDER *begins to laugh.*]

BILLY: We'll be witnesses . . .

ALEXANDER: Maybe Mickey wants to die along with you, but I don't. Look, Mickey, I need to talk to you. You're lettin' him come between us? We mixed our blood. We took an oath.

YOUNG MICKEY: You broke that oath when you became one of them.

ALEXANDER: I never broke no oath to you. Square bizness. We was supposed to be forever. Ace boons . . . But no, you act this way? Treat me like a pussy that's been gang-fucked? You let the likes of him come between us, Nigga?

YOUNG MICKEY: Ain't nobody afraid of you.

ALEXANDER: You ain't supposed to be afraid of me . . . you're supposed to be my main man you stupid Uncle Tom-aintcha-mama-on-the-pancake box, motherfucker. What you learn from that faggot Daniel so you can poke your friend here up his Kosher ass?

YOUNG MICKEY: Go home.

LEXANDER: Fuck you. [*Pause.*] Look, man, I wanna rap to you about . . .

OUNG MICKEY: I don't care . . . just go.

LEXANDER: My friend! Yo' ass is mine.

[ALEXANDER *leaves. Pause.*]

ILLY: Forget him.

OUNG MICKEY: What???

ILLY: He's trash.

OUNG MICKEY: Billy, you don't know him well enough . . .

ILLY: He's a creep, and . . .

OUNG MICKEY: Shut your mouth. Sometimes it's like you think you know everything. The two of yous are like that . . . think you know everything . . .

ILLY: I ain't like him . . .

OUNG MICKEY: Don't you understand, he was scared . . .

ILLY: He was spying on us for that scumbag Prince.

OUNG MICKEY: He was scared, man!

ILLY: Then if he was scared . . . why's you make him go?

OUNG MICKEY: 'Cause I wasn't sure 'til he went away.

ILLY: C'mon.

OUNG MICKEY: Where?

ILLY: To get my father, we're going to the police.

OUNG MICKEY: Billy, I'm not going to . . .

BILLY: The neighborhood will finally be rid of these guys.

YOUNG MICKEY: You rat on the Prince and you'll choke on the cheese...

BILLY: You gotta be true, Mickey... like my Dad says...

YOUNG MICKEY: He's not talking about something like this

BILLY: He's talkin' about life.

YOUNG MICKEY: Well, if you want to lose yours, rat on the Prince.

[BILLY *starts to leave.*]

BILLY: I ain't afraid. Maybe you're not behind me, but my dad will be.

[BILLY *leaves.* YOUNG MICKEY *looks after him. Lights fade.*]

SCENE 2

Lights up on BILLY *and* MR. KORNBLUM.

MR. KORNBLUM: No, no... no way. Forget it! You hear me William?

BILLY: Then just tell me I'm wrong.

MR. KORNBLUM: You want me to say you're wrong? [*Pause.*] You're wrong.

BILLY: What about the truth, Pop?

MR. KORNBLUM: You listen to me, mister... I want the truth...

BILLY: You're always talking about being true . . . whether it's hitting a baseball or life . . .

MR. KORNBLUM: William, there's nothing to discuss.

BILLY: Pop, we're talking about a cop . . .

MR. KORNBLUM: Look, someone probably already told the cops what happened.

BILLY: That's what Mickey said.

MR. KORNBLUM: See . . . he should know. He understands the schwartzer mentality . . .

BILLY: What?

[*Pause.*]

MR. KORNBLUM: Uhh . . . You know what I mean . . .

BILLY: No, Pop . . . I don't know what you mean.

MR. KORNBLUM: I mean . . . he knows that someone in the park . . . some grownup will get involved . . .

BILLY: But what if they don't, Pop? Huh? There was only kids there . . . white ones too, for your information. So what if they don't?

MR. KORNBLUM: Then . . . they don't . . .

BILLY: Pop, you and Grandma . . . you always taught me that all life is sacred . . .

MR. KORNBLUM: That's right . . . and nothing is more sacred to me than your life, William . . . I've lost a wife, I'm not going to lose a son . . . Do you understand? Don't you understand that I don't want you hurt by those neanderthal hoodlums? They'll be out off jail in a day. They'l put a bullet in you. And there's the end of my world. I'n a dead man. Do you understand? I mean, when you mother was dying...

BILLY: I understand, Pop...

MR. KORNBLUM: Do ya?...

BILLY: Yeah... and it ain't good enough, Pop.

[MR. KORNBLUM *slaps his son. Pause.*]

BILLY: Gee, Pop, you should join Spectre... you'd fit right in

MR. KORNBLUM: You requested that, young man.

BILLY: I thought you treasured the truth. Always talking abou how the Jews in Europe took too much crap, and here you are...

MR. KORNBLUM: This isn't Germany, William...

BILLY: Thank God it isn't, Pop... 'cause if you're afraid of a bunch of bullies... then I'm scared to think what kind o coward you'da been over there.

[MR. KORNBLUM *draws closer.*]

BILLY: [*Cont'd.*] Slap me again, Pop. It ain't gonna change a thing. You slap my face a hundred times... you're still a blowhard. You're still a coward. You preach the truth without even believing in it... My Pop, my Pop, my swel truth-sayer Pop... with a spine of a shrimp... which ain't Kosher.

MR. KORNBLUM: William... Billy...

[BILLY *walks away. Lights fade slowly on* MR. KORNBLUM.]

MR. KORNBLUM: [*Cont'd.*] Billy . . . son, let's talk about this . . . BILLY!

[*Blackout.*]

SCENE 3

Lights up on THE PRINCE.

THE PRINCE: James Bond movies are fly 'cause the dudes he be fightin' . . . mainly the Spectre gang, well, they the baddest of the bad . . . and I dig 'em 'cause they know it don't matter. See, I believe that SPECTRE could kick James Bond, that faggoty talkin' Englishman, I believe they could kick his ass, and do . . . but they change the story . . . the Dude with the cat . . . he treats his people right . . . but they fuck up and gotta pay the price.

[*Lights up on* ALEXANDER *with a noose around his neck. The rope is tossed over a branch.* ODD JOB *pulls the other end of the rope while* ALEXANDER *dangles hanging.*]

THE PRINCE: Why you run?

[ALEXANDER *struggles.*]

THE PRINCE: [*Cont'd.*] Nobody in Spectre runs . . . Why you run?

[THE PRINCE *signals for* ODD JOB *to let* ALEXANDER *down.* ODD JOB *does.*]

THE PRINCE: [*Cont'd.*] I say, why you run?

ALEXANDER: I . . . I . . . I . . .

[ALEXANDER *coughs.* THE PRINCE *signals and* ODD JOB *pulls the rope leaving* ALEXANDER *dangling once again.*]

THE PRINCE: I wish I had one of them trap doors like Blo- feld . . . with an alligator waitin' to chomp your ass up. I'd say #1 stand over there.

[THE PRINCE *signals for* ODD JOB *to give the rope some slack.*]

THE PRINCE: [*Cont'd.*] I'm only fifteen and nobody messes with me. What's it gonna be like when I'm twenty? . . Why'd you run? [*Pause.*]
String his ass again.

ALEXANDER: No, wait . . . wait . . .

THE PRINCE: What it be like? Why you run when you know Spectre don't gotta run?

ALEXANDER: I . . . I . . . I was spyin'.

THE PRINCE: Spyin'? Do I look like Laurel and Hardy and shit. Hang 'im. Hang 'im high!

ALEXANDER: No, no . . . square bizness . . . on the up and up . .

THE PRINCE: What you rappin'?

ALEXANDER: When you offed that pig . . .

ODD JOB: He's jivin', he's jivin'. Let's just hang his ass.

ALEXANDER: That's my job as your #1 . . . to look out. I followed them . . .

ODD JOB: That little rat Mickey . . .

ALEXANDER: No, no, Mickey's cool . . . real cool . . . if we can get him away from that Jew-boy. It's the Jew-boy . . . he wants to go to the cops.

IE PRINCE: Let him down.

[ODD JOB *does.*]

IE PRINCE: [*Cont'd.*] That's a dead Jew. He been to the cops yet?

.EXANDER: No, but he's tryin' to push Mickey to go with him.

IE PRINCE: What Mickey say?

.EXANDER: No way.

DD JOB: What about the fag?

IE PRINCE: Don't worry about him. I've got something to gag him up. Believe me. [*Pause.*]

All right then. I'll spare you . . . and Mickey too . . . and if he keeps his mouth shut . . .

DD JOB: What about the Jew, Your Grace?

HE PRINCE: Death!

[THE PRINCE *exits.*]

DD JOB: Death! Death!

[ODD JOB *exits.* ALEXANDER *watches as they leave. Lights fade.*]

SCENE 4

The woods. DANIEL *is dressed in a suit. He carries severa music books with him. He is humming a classical tune.* THE PRINCE *remains hidden, as* ODD JOB *comes forward.*

ODD JOB: Hey . . .

DANIEL: Yes?

ODD JOB: What the fuck is that . . . "yes" . . . say it like you fro the Bronx . . . say "yeah" . . . only faggots from Queens ar Staten Island say "yes" 'cause they ain't got no balls.

DANIEL: Yes . . .

ODD JOB: I'll call you my little Queenie . . . You wanna be m little Queenie?

[THE PRINCE *walks up. He blows kisses at* DANIEL. *He and* ODD JOB *draw closer to* DANIEL.]

DANIEL: What do you want?

THE PRINCE: What do you want?

DANIEL: Look, I'm going to be late for my concert.

THE PRINCE: How'd you like to play my flute?

[ODD JOB *starts to laugh.* THE PRINCE *viciously pushes* DANIEL *to his knees. Now* ODD JOB *unzips his pants in front of* DANIEL*'s face.*]

ODD JOB: Play me a song . . .

THE PRINCE: Blow, punk, blow.

DANIEL: Why are you doing this to me?

HE PRINCE: You supposed to like this. You a punk! C'mon, let's run a train on this bitch.

[THE PRINCE *unzips his pants. He starts to try to undo* DANIEL*'s pants.* DANIEL *turns,* THE PRINCE *slaps him.*]

HE PRINCE: Don't worry about what I'm doin' back here . . . just start smokin' Odd Job's pole.

[*As* THE PRINCE *starts to unbuckle* DANIEL*'s pants,* ODD JOB *brings his crotch closer to* DANIEL*'s face. Suddenly,* DANIEL *punches* ODD JOB *in the balls.* ODD JOB *falls to the ground.* DANIEL *hits* THE PRINCE *with an elbow to the stomach.* DANIEL *then gets up and tries to run.* THE PRINCE *is not hurt, in fact, he seems to enjoy this. He chases after* DANIEL *and corners him.*]

HE PRINCE: You got balls, huh, sweetboy?

ANIEL: I just want to go to my concert . . .

HE PRINCE: You're a wild one. Like to fight before you give it up.

[DANIEL *tries to hit* THE PRINCE, *but* THE PRINCE *knocks him down.*]

HE PRINCE: You want some more? . . . Damn, you got some balls. I give you that. You actually tried to punch out the Prince.

[ODD JOB *is up now.*]

ANIEL: Why are you picking on me? I didn't do anything to you.

HE PRINCE: What are you yip yappin' about?

DANIEL: I'm not the enemy. We don't have time to hurt ea other no more.

THE PRINCE: Ain't that some shit? Then you don't kno nothin' 'bout that cop, do ya?

DANIEL: No, no, no.

THE PRINCE: Then I don't wanna hear a motherfucking thin but you screamin' with delight when I lay my pipe on yo

ODD JOB: That li'l punk motherfucker.

[ODD JOB *kicks* DANIEL.]

THE PRINCE: Come on, let's give 'im what he likes.

[DANIEL *tries to fight, but they beat him to the ground. Then, as* ODD JOB *holds him,* THE PRINCE *pulls* DANIEL*'s pants down.*

Blackout.]

SCENE 5

The concert hall. YOUNG MICKEY *sits at the edge of the stage.* DANIEL *comes in. His clothes are in disarray.*

YOUNG MICKEY: I told you I'd be here.

DANIEL: First we'll go with the Mozart piece . . . Just in cas you have trouble reading the music, I'll nod my head the end of each page . . .

YOUNG MICKEY: Like we practiced . . .

DANIEL: Right.

[YOUNG MICKEY *looks at* DANIEL.]

OUNG MICKEY: What happened to your clothes?

ANIEL: I tripped when I cut through the woods.

[*Pause.*]

OUNG MICKEY: You sure you're all right?

[YOUNG MICKEY *begins to dust the dirt from* DANIEL*'s shirt.*]

ANIEL: Don't touch me!

OUNG MICKEY: What's eatin' you?

ANIEL: I'm sorry, I...

OUNG MICKEY: What happened to you? You didn't trip in the woods?

ANIEL: Yeah...I tripped all right. Over The Prince and Odd Job.

OUNG MICKEY: They beat you up?

ANIEL: They did something worse...

OUNG MICKEY: What? They what?

ANIEL: I tease you sometimes...I know. And I act like I know it all. But the only thing I really know is my music. I would never hurt you...

OUNG MICKEY: I know that, Daniel.

ANIEL: I can't go on tonight.

OUNG MICKEY: What do you mean you can't go on? The audience is just comin' back from intermission.

ANIEL: I can't...

YOUNG MICKEY: You're always tellin' me about overcomin obstacles . . . Well, you just gotta do that . . .

DANIEL: Why?

YOUNG MICKEY: 'Cause I heard these others play, and the suck, you're the best, Daniel, and . . .

DANIEL: Just leave it alone, Mickey!

VOICE OF THE M.C.: The next contestant is sixteen-year-ol Daniel Van Drake.

YOUNG MICKEY: Daniel, let 'em know how you feel.

[YOUNG MICKEY *goes to the piano with* DANIEL. *There is applause.* DANIEL *is still a bit shaken and unsure as the applause dies down.* YOUNG MICKEY *sits next to him and turns the first page of the composition.*

Long pause.

DANIEL *begins playing a Mozart piece. First shakily, but, by the time* YOUNG MICKEY *turns the page for him, he is confident. The lights fade slowly on this.*]

SCENE 6

Lights up on YOUNG MICKEY *and* BILLY. YOUNG MICKEY *has a stickball bat in hand and* BILLY *is pitching a Spaldeen that is invisible to the audience. They silently mime the stickball game "Strikeout" as* BIG MICKEY *enters.* YOUNG MICKEY *wears his Pirate cap, while* BILLY *wears an Oriole cap.*

BIG MICKEY: Strikeout was a stickball game with the fas pitching of a Spaldeen . . . All the guys who loved base ball . . . when they couldn't play hard ball or softball played Strikeout. Now in Brooklyn they called it fast pitch, and in Manhattan it was Pitch in, but everybody knows they don't know anything about baseball. I guess that's why the Dodgers and the Giants left. Anyway, for 69 cents you could get a stickball bat in various colors with the end taped, and you could get a genuine Spaldeen for about 35 cents . . . The big strikeout courts were behind P.S. 112. There were about seven or eight chalked boxes. If you pitched in the box it was a strike . . . outside the box it was a ball and . . .

[BILLY *pitches.* YOUNG MICKEY *swings and hits.*]

)UNG MICKEY: There's a line drive by Clemente! . . .

[BILLY *dives for the ball.*]

)UNG MICKEY: [*Cont'd.*] It gets between Belanger and Robinson . . . Base hit!!! [YOUNG MICKEY *makes the sound of the crowd.*]

The bases are loaded . . . it's the bottom of the ninth . . . and out of the on-deck circle comes that man . . . Willie Stargell . . .

LLY: You gotta bat left handed . . .

)UNG MICKEY: I know that . . . Stargel's left handed . . .

LLY: Robinson comes over to talk to McNally . . .

)UNG MICKEY: Who's in the bullpen?

LLY: Nobody . . . McNally's still pitching a shutout, folks . . .

)UNG MICKEY: Not for long, folks . . . the bases are loaded . . .

BILLY: It's three nothin' Orioles . . .

YOUNG MICKEY: With Clemente on first, Alley and Alou c second and third . . .

BILLY: Robinson pats McNally on the tusch . . . and McNal steps on the mound

YOUNG MICKEY: Stargell steps into the batter's box . . .

BILLY: Left handed . . . left handed . . .

YOUNG MICKEY: I know . . . I know . . .

[YOUNG MICKEY *bats left handed.*]

BILLY: McNally winds and the pitch . . .

[YOUNG MICKEY *swings.*]

BILLY: [*Cont'd.*] Stargell swings and misses . . . Strike one . as Stargell shakes his head in disbelief . . . now McNal goes into the stretch position . . . He looks over to first . he winds, rocks and deals . . .

[BILLY *pitches.* YOUNG MICKEY *does not swing.*]

BILLY: [*Cont'd.*] Strike two on the outside corner.

[BILLY *catches the ball as it bounces back off the wall.*]

YOUNG MICKEY: Git outta here . . . that was a ball.

BILLY: You kiddin' me? Didn't you see that chalk exploc when the ball hit the wall . . .

[BILLY *looks at the ball and smiles.*]

BILLY: [*Cont'd.*] There's chalk all over . . .

YOUNG MICKEY: Throw it and let me see.

[BILLY *brings it to him instead.*]

YOUNG MICKEY: [*Cont'd.*] That's old chalk.

BILLY: It's not.

YOUNG MICKEY: You wipe that ball off.

BILLY: Always do . . .

YOUNG MICKEY: Not in this life you don't . . .

[BILLY *walks back to the mound.*]

BILLY: You're just a sore loser . . .

YOUNG MICKEY: You put it in the box, you little twerp . . . have some balls . . . Pirates are a National League team . . . we like fastballs. The pitchers challenge you in the N.L. . . . instead of throwing that slick stuff . . . Gimme a fastball and it's ovah . . .

BILLY: Give you my slow-sinking-double-clutch-knuckle-curve and it's ovah!

YOUNG MICKEY: A faggot pitch for a faggot league.

BILLY: Yeah, the faggot league of Mickey Mantle, Brooks Robinson, Harmon Killebrew, Al Kaline, Carl Yastremski . . .

YOUNG MICKEY: That's right . . . against the challenge league of Willie Mays, Roberto Clemente, Willie McCovey, Juan Marichai . . .

BILLY: Denny McClain!

YOUNG MICKEY: Bob Gibson!

BILLY: The National League sucks!

YOUNG MICKEY: American League is a puff league . . .

BILLY: Get up to bat and I'll show you puff league . . .

YOUNG MICKEY: Only way you get me out . . . you throw me one of them American League puff balls . . . you give me a man's pitch.

BILLY: Shut up and get to bat . . .

YOUNG MICKEY: Who you tellin' to shut up? I'm gonna hit a line drive right in your mouth . . .

BILLY: Good, and it'll be an out . . . I take 'em as I get 'em . . .

[YOUNG MICKEY *waits for the pitch.*]

BILLY: [*Cont'd.*] McNally looks for the signal from Andy Echebarren, he shakes off the sign.

YOUNG MICKEY: That's right, ladies and gentlemen, it was a signal for fastball, but McNally shook it off. After the game, McNally and Robinson will go have cream puffs and tea. Stargell and Clemente? Why, of course, they'll have a Schlitz.

BILLY: And run over some little ol' lady from Pasadena because they were driving drunk.

YOUNG MICKEY: Roberto Clemente don't drive drunk!!! Brooks Robinson takes it up the ass!!!

BILLY: The Pirate bench is yelling profanities that we cannot repeat . . . But the Baltimore team are cool professionals who are unflappable . . . McNally goes into the stretch . . . he rocks . . . he deals . . .

[BILLY *pitches.* YOUNG MICKEY *swings. He hits the ball and watches as it ascends a majestic height.* BILLY *turns and watches the ball.*]

YOUNG MICKEY: That ball is deep, deep . . .

BILLY: But it's curvin' foul . . . foul . . .

YOUNG MICKEY: But deep . . . deep . . . still fair . . . and high . . . The ball is outta here!!!! On the roof!!!! Fourteen freakin' stories . . . A grand slam for Willie Stargell!!!

[YOUNG MICKEY *starts to run imaginary bases in a home-run trot.*]

YOUNG MICKEY: [*Cont'd.*] Stargell suckered McNally into throwing a fastball and the ball game is over. The Pirates win 4 to 3. What a shot!

BILLY: Stop showing off, hot dog . . .

YOUNG MICKEY: You show off all the time.

BILLY: You're a hot dogger like all those National Leaguers. Mays and Clemente with their basket catches . . . they're not in the jungle . . . they don't need baskets . . .

YOUNG MICKEY: The jungle? Tell you what, I'd like to see Mantle or Robinson in the N.L. . . . they'd never make it. American League's a prejudiced league . . .

BILLY: Yeah, yeah, yeah . . . All I know is, as good as the Pirates are, they can't even make it to the World Series.

YOUNG MICKEY: All I know is, I just beat your ass . . .

BILLY: I beat you three days in a row last week . . .

YOUNG MICKEY: But this is this week.

BILLY: Yeah, yeah, yeah . . . good shot . . . better get to the roof and get my ball . . .

YOUNG MICKEY: Hey . . . your Dad take you to the precinct?

BILLY: No.

YOUNG MICKEY: I knew he wasn't gonna let you go to the cops.

BILLY: The hell with the truth.

YOUNG MICKEY: Billy, he don't care about the truth . . .

BILLY: Damn right . . .

YOUNG MICKEY: He just don't wanna see you hurt. Can't you see that, you jerk? If my father were still alive, I'd obey him even if I thought he was wrong.

BILLY: Yeah, screw the truth. The truth is, you're both scared of a bunch of bullies. The whole neighborhood is. Nobody cares about that cop. I keep seein' it over and over . . . in the back . . . that looney tunes wacko didn't even give him a chance. My father . . . my best friend . . . tell me I'm wrong when I know I'm right . . . People you count on the most . . . One's a scared little Jew, and the other's a nigger.

[BIG MICKEY *cringes.* YOUNG MICKEY *belts* BILLY *who falls to the ground.*

Pause.]

BILLY: It don't mean nothin' if you can beat me. Can you beat the Prince? Can you walk through the doors of the 47th Precinct with me and beat the Prince? . . .

YOUNG MICKEY: Why should I walk in with you? Who wants to walk with you anyway? You know, Alexander's right. I'm just a nigger to you... Jew-boy...

[BILLY *starts to get up, but* YOUNG MICKEY *pushes him back down. He hovers over* BILLY *as if he's about to hit him again. Then he leaves.*

BILLY *sits there alone as the lights fade.*]

SCENE 7

Lights up on BIG MICKEY.

BIG MICKEY: Billy and I didn't see each other for the next few days. I didn't speak to him in class... And I missed two days of baseball practice just to avoid him. I thought he was wrong... that he should keep his mouth shut, listen to his father. That's what I thought... until it all went down... None of us would ever be the same again.

[*Lights down.*

Martin Luther King's last speech, the "Mountain Top" begins to play. MOTHER *enters.*]

MOTHER: Mickey! Mickey! Where are you? I know you hear me, boy. Get down here and witness history and watch Dr. King work his mojo on America. Listen to him weave his words... I strut his stuff... James Brown is bad, but Martin is baaad. He got soul and he superbad. Get down here, boy. Get down here. Mickey, come live history. Hear Reverend King in Memphis. Watch us rise!

[*Blackout.*

Shots are heard in the dark.
Lights up on BIG MICKEY.]

BIG MICKEY: That very next day . . . the Bronx died . . . it never has recovered from this day. It was not the beginning of the end, but the end. You see . . . a disciple of peace dies in Memphis and it leads to rage in the Bronx. Come 3 o'clock, if you were white, your ass was grass. Nobody black stood up when Spectre Gestapo'd the neighborhood supermarket. They destroyed it. Nobody black said a damn thing when Milton Friedman got the shit beat out of him as he opened his bakery one morning. No one black, of good conscience, said a fucking word . . . And in the end, when we had no neighborhood supermarket . . . or bakery of fine pastries . . . they only moaned that familiar, sick, sorry, blame everybody but-your-fuckin'-self whine!

[*Lights up on* BILLY *carrying his books. Yelling and screaming is heard. General riot using all company members.*

BILLY *runs to the other side of the stage and runs into* YOUNG MICKEY. BILLY *backs away. He is afraid* YOUNG MICKEY *is going to strike him.*]

YOUNG MICKEY: Hey, Billy, I . . .

BILLY: Get away from me!!!

[BILLY *drops his books and runs to the other side of the stage where he bumps into* THE PRINCE. *He bolts again and runs into* ODD JOB. *He runs again and runs into* ALEXANDER.]

THE PRINCE: Jesus . . . then Malcolm . . . now King . . . and, of course, me. The Prince.

ODD JOB: Let's roast this little Jew pigette.

THE PRINCE: Yeah, I'm in the mood for the kill . . .

ODD JOB: The kill . . .

ALEXANDER: Beat his ass so he'll remember not to go to the cops.

THE PRINCE: Hey, this ain't about no beating. This is about shuttin' up a squealin' pig.

[THE PRINCE *pulls out his gun.* THE PRINCE *and* ODD JOB *draw closer to* BILLY. ALEXANDER *stands there, not quite sure what to do.* YOUNG MICKEY *drops his books and runs across the stage.*]

YOUNG MICKEY: Noooooooo!!!

[BILLY *sees* YOUNG MICKEY *coming at him. He covers himself up as if expecting to be hit by* YOUNG MICKEY. YOUNG MICKEY *knocks the gun from* THE PRINCE*'s hand.*]

THE PRINCE: You touched the Prince. I'm gonna off you first.

[ODD JOB *picks up the gun and hits* YOUNG MICKEY *in the back of the head.* YOUNG MICKEY *slumps to the ground.* THE PRINCE *takes the gun from* ODD JOB.]

ALEXANDER: You said you wasn't gonna hurt Mickey.

THE PRINCE: He got in my way.

[BILLY *bends down to take care of* YOUNG MICKEY .]

ALEXANDER: Okay, man . . . he's learned his lesson.

THE PRINCE: Yeah, but this little yarmulke wearing son of a bitch ain't.

ALEXANDER: You ain't gonna say nothin' about what happened in the park, are you, Billy?

BILLY: I don't wanna die... I don't want Mickey to die... I just wanna get Mickey home. I won't say nothin'.

[THE PRINCE *aims at* BILLY.]

ALEXANDER: You don't have to do this. We can let him go.

THE PRINCE: When the fuck you start wearin' the balls around here?

ALEXANDER: I just don't want you to go off... like you did with that cop.

THE PRINCE: Just hope I don't go off on you. Now 'cause I feel in a good mood, I'll let Mickey go... but Jew-boy...

[THE PRINCE *is still aiming at* BILLY.

BILLY *places* YOUNG MICKEY*'s head gently down. He rises and backs away.*]

BILLY: You just don't give a shit... You're a fucking animal.

ALEXANDER: Hey, man... Prince... don't do this. Like, I know the cop and all... You lost your temper. But this is cold-blooded.

THE PRINCE: He's a fuckin' Jew-boy.

ALEXANDER: He's just a kid, man.

THE PRINCE: Fuck around here and you next, bitch!

[ALEXANDER *looks at* BILLY. *He smiles.*]

ALEXANDER: I guess you right, Jew-boy.

BILLY: [*Backing away slowly, nervously.*] Huh?

ALEXANDER: The motherfucker is an animal.

[*Suddenly,* ALEXANDER *grabs* THE PRINCE *by the head, he brings his own knee up and smashes* THE PRINCE*'s head into it.* THE PRINCE *collapses to the ground. Severely dazed, he drops the gun.*

ALEXANDER *goes to* THE PRINCE.]

ALEXANDER: You know what we gonna do?

BILLY: What?

ALEXANDER: We're gonna get Mickey home, and then you and me are gonna go to the 47th Precinct. We're gonna tell 'em what happened in the park... We ain't gotta be afraid of these guys...

YOUNG MICKEY: Help me up...

ALEXANDER: Are you okay?

[ODD JOB *goes after the gun.* BIG MICKEY *is frantic.* ALEXANDER *sees* ODD JOB *going for the gun.* ALEXANDER *turns and sees* ODD JOB. *They race for the gun, but* ODD JOB *is closer.* ODD JOB *points the gun at* ALEXANDER.]

BIG MICKEY AND YOUNG MICKEY: No!!!!

[YOUNG MICKEY *tries to go to* ALEXANDER, *but* BILLY *pulls him down to the ground.* ODD JOB *fires.* BIG MICKEY *turns and sees* ALEXANDER *stand for a few beats.*]

ALEXANDER: Mickey...

[ALEXANDER *falls.*]

YOUNG MICKEY: Alexander.

[ODD JOB *grabs* THE PRINCE *and helps him off.*
YOUNG MICKEY *and* BILLY *go to the fallen* ALEXANDER.
YOUNG MICKEY *holds him in his arms.*
YOUNG MICKEY *begins rocking* ALEXANDER *in his arms.*]

YOUNG MICKEY: Alexander . . . Alexander . . . you're going t(be OK. It's gonna be OK. Stay with me. Somebody ge some help!!

[BILLY *runs for help.*]

YOUNG MICKEY: Help's coming. It's gonna be OK. You'r(gonna be OK, Alex . . .

[ALEXANDER *lies dead. Church bells toll.*
Lights.]

SCENE 8

Lights up on BIG MICKEY.

BIG MICKEY: Billy and I were pallbearers at the funeral. Foı the first thirteen years of my life, death was something very vague. An obscure stranger who was not a part o my reality. I lost my father, then Alexander, in a period of four months. Death had established an unwanted intimacy with me.

[*Lights up on the* MOTHER *and* MR. KORNBLUM. *They are dressed in black.*]

MOTHER: Feel like everything's dead . . .

MR. KORNBLUM: He was just a baby . . . babies with guns.

MOTHER: I didn't know I had such a well of tears in me. Mickey's daddy . . . well, he was an old man, but I flooded the house. This time I can't stop at all.

[MR. KORNBLUM *gives her a handkerchief.*]

MOTHER: [*Cont'd.*] In less than a day . . . King and Alexander . . . when I'm not cryin' for one I'm cryin' for the other.

MR. KORNBLUM: They gotta do something to get this neighborhood back together.

[*They go off together.*

BILLY *and* YOUNG MICKEY *enter. They are wearing black suits.*]

BILLY: I always thought a casket would be heavy. But six of us . . . six kids . . . we lifted it like it was nothing.

YOUNG MICKEY: I thought it was kind of heavy.

BILLY: It wasn't heavy.

YOUNG MICKEY: To me it was. I couldn't wait to put it down. I was thinkin', "gosh, Alexander, you sure are heavy."

BILLY: I'm moving.

[*Pause.*]

YOUNG MICKEY: You're just trying to psych my mind.

BILLY: I ain't psyching you.

[*Pause.*]

YOUNG MICKEY: Where you moving to.

BILLY: Larchmont.

YOUNG MICKEY: It's your Dad, huh?

BILLY: He says it's not like it used to be around here. He says the whole city is turning into a dump. He's scared of what might happen next. [*Pause.*]

So am I. Kids aren't supposed to have bullets in them. Their friends shouldn't have to carry their coffins.

YOUNG MICKEY: Well, I'm gonna get out of here too one day... away from all this. Like when my mother takes me to the shows and the museums... Those buildings with doormen. I'm gonna have one of them apartments. And if I have kids... they ain't never gonna have to deal with something like this.

BILLY: How you gonna do that?

YOUNG MICKEY: I'm gonna be somebody. I ain't gonna stay here forever.

[*Lights up on* DANIEL. *He begins to play his piano. An R. Nathaniel Dett piece, "The Place Where the Rainbow Ends." He plays it low.*]

YOUNG MICKEY: [*Cont'd.*] Baseball ain't gonna be fun anymore without Brooks Robinson's nephew beside me.

BILLY: He ain't my uncle.

YOUNG MICKEY: Yes he is.

BILLY: You know he isn't.

[*Pause.*]

YOUNG MICKEY: Yeah... I know... but it was fun pretending.

BILLY: We're too old to pretend.

[BILLY *walks away. The* MOTHER *enters. She goes to* YOUNG MICKEY.]

MOTHER: You're just the opposite of me, Mickey. Nothing touches you. It's a sin for someone to be so cold. Or is it that there's a drought in your well of tears? You're all I've got in the world. They're going to have to hire people to cry at my funeral 'cause my child surely won't.

[YOUNG MICKEY *begins to cry.* DANIEL *puts his arm around him.*]

DANIEL: It's okay. Go ahead and let it run.

[*The lights lower on* YOUNG MICKEY *and* DANIEL.

The DOCTOR *enters.* BIG MICKEY *turns and sees him. Their eyes meet for a beat.*]

BIG MICKEY: Is it over?

DOCTOR: He's in recovery.

BIG MICKEY: Will he make it?

DOCTOR: I'm not sure. I don't have the answer to that at this point... It's too early to tell. But he has a chance.

BIG MICKEY: A good chance?

DOCTOR: He has a chance.

[*Pause. The* DOCTOR *leaves.*]

BIG MICKEY: He's going to be all right. That's what my heart tells me. We'll play catch in the park again... He'll let me win at chess... And I'll yell at him for any number of things that a parent yells at a child for... I'm going to find a safe place. Now I know some of you think there is no such place. You probably think I'm naive. But I've got to believe such a place exists. You see, my wife could be next, my baby . . . me. Let's face it . . . the melting pot has faded into antiquity with the sixty-nine cents stickball bat. [*Pause.*]

I lived high above it all. I took pity upon them. Upon them. As if they were helpless victims. Well, the tables have turned, and I, you . . . we're the victims . . . of ourselves . . . because we don't have the guts to take back our civilization. [*Pause.*]

I don't want to bury my children. I want it as it was meant to be . . . That when they are in middle-age, my children will stand over the graves of their parents.

END OF PLAY

I AM A MAN

A New Play

by OyamO

"A GRIPPING NEW PLAY BY OYAMO..."

—WILBORN HAMPTON
The New York Times

"A struggle not only between striking workers and city officials, but also between the violent "by any means necessary" tactics associated with Malcolm X and the passive nonviolence of King... **ENGROSSINGLY DRAMATIZED BY OYAMO"**

—ROBERT BRUSTEIN
The New Republic

OyamO's powerful new play depicts the events around a strike in Memphis in 1968, leading up to the assasination of Martin Luther King. I AM A MAN is forthcoming as a special presentation on HBO, following its acclaimed runs in New York, Chicago and at the Arena Stage in Washington D.C.

OyamO's work has been performed at the Yale Repertory Theater, Manhattan Theatre Club, The Kennedy Center, The Public Theatre, Negro Ensemble Company, The Working Theatre, Ensemble Studio Theatre, Eureka Theatre (San Francisco) and Theatre Emory (Atlanta)

Paper•ISBN 1-55783-211-0 • $6.95
Performance rights available from APPLAUSE

GHOST IN THE MACHINE

A New Play

by David Gilman

"A devilishly clever puzzler of a comedy...it traps us in a web of uncertainty till we begin to wecond guess with the characters."

—Jan Stewart, *New York Newsday*

"A vastly entertaining whodunit, a chess gane with human pieces that does not limit itself...Gilman teases us with philosophical questions on the nature of reality..."

—Laurie Winer, *The Los Angeles Times*

"Atight theatrical puzzle, the play echoes both the menacing personal relationships at the center of Harold Pinter's work and the complex mathematical equations that animate Tom Stoppard...but it is also very much of its own thing."

—Hedy Weiss, *The Chicago Sun Times*

Ghost in the the Machine begins with a common situation-that of a missing fifty dollar bill-and spins it into intriguing questions of probability, chance and the complexities of musical composition: illusion and reality.

Paper•ISBN 1-55783-228-5• $6.95
Performance rights available from APPLAUSE